Animal Mandala Adult Coloring Book Vol 3

60 Entertaining Stress Relieving Animal Patterns

By Omar Johnson

Get Your Free Mandala

Visit

ADULTCOLORINGBOOKSFORYOU.COM

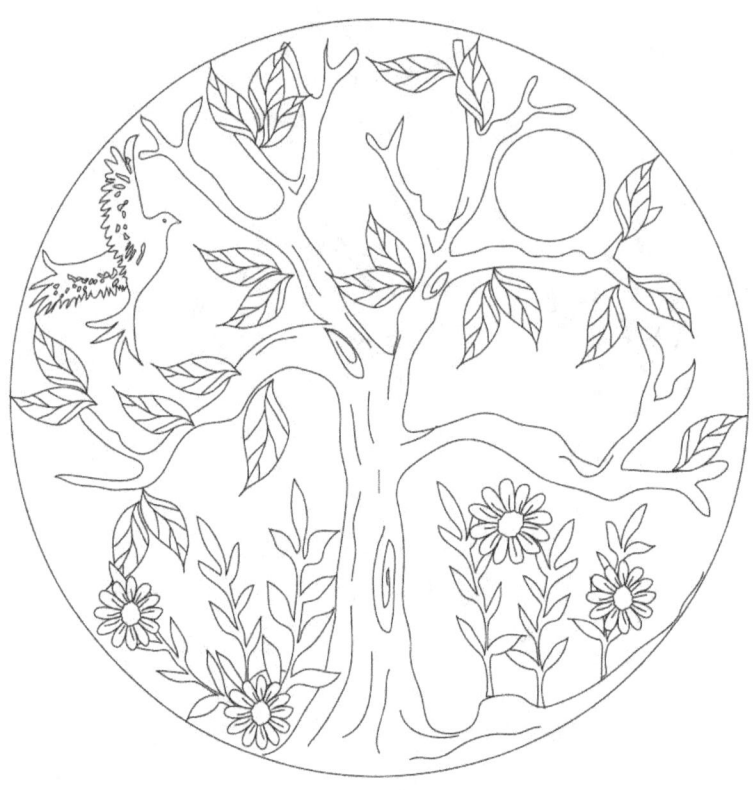

Make Profits Easy LLC Publishing
profitsdaily123@aol.com
Copyright 2015

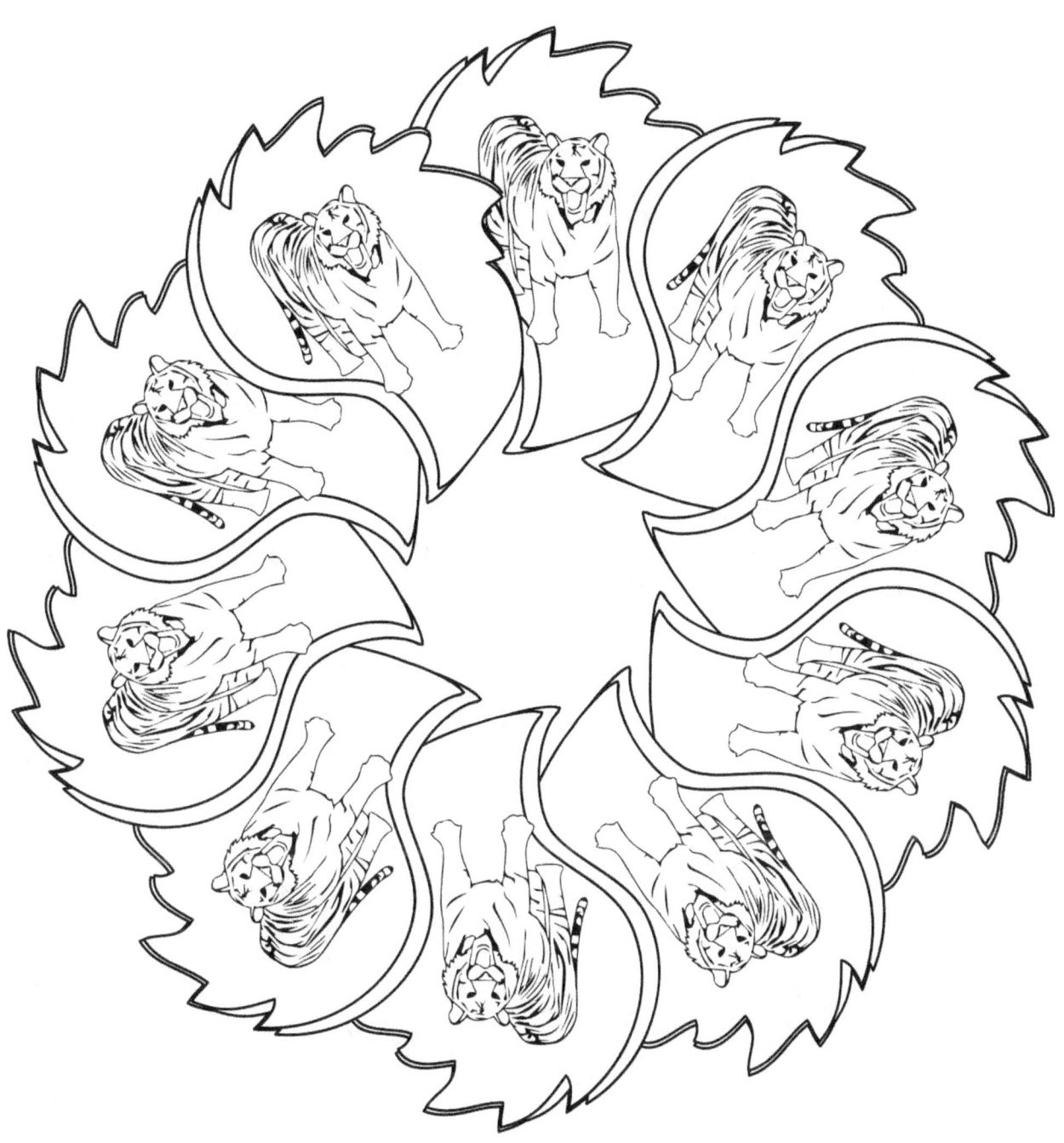

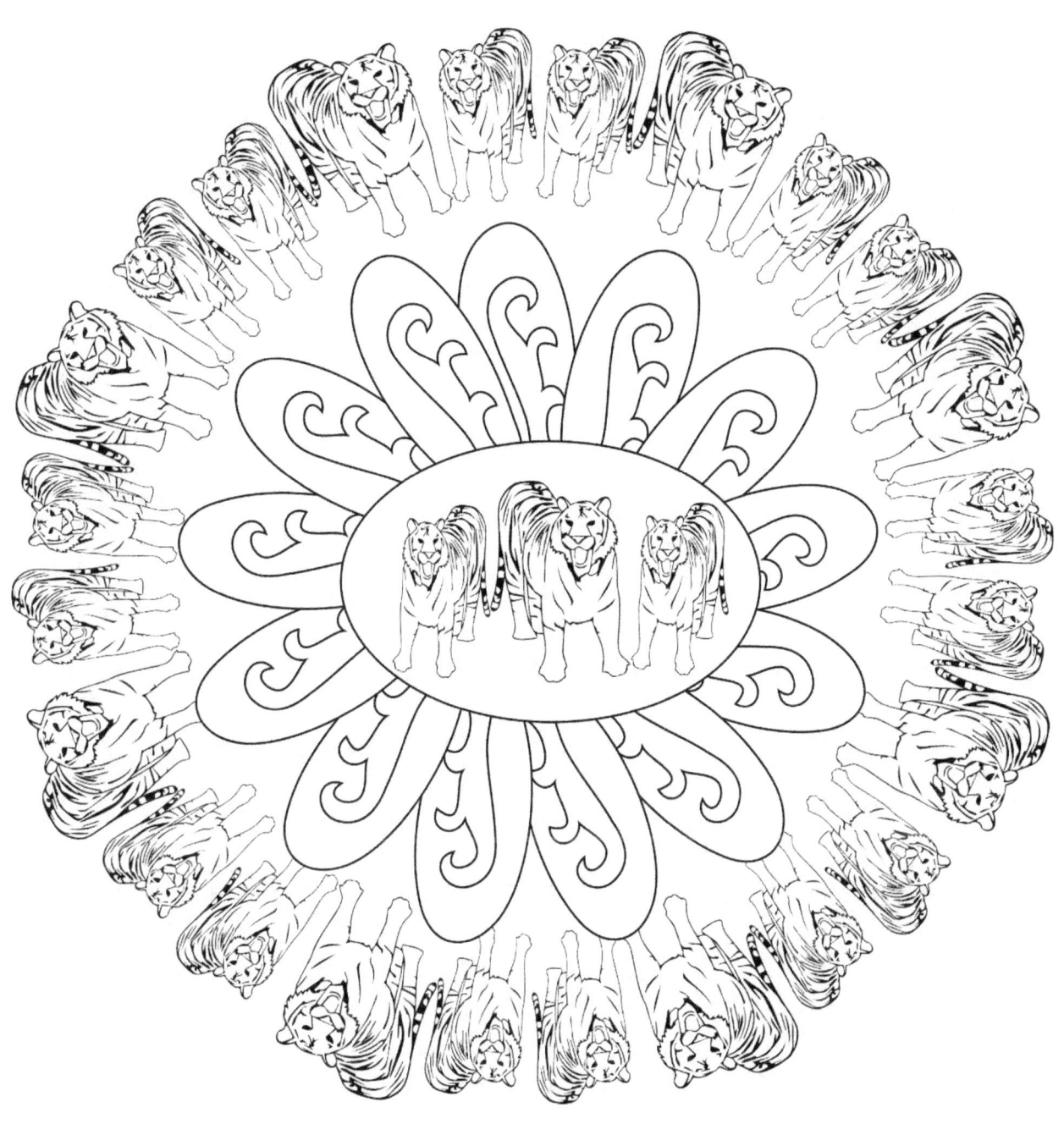

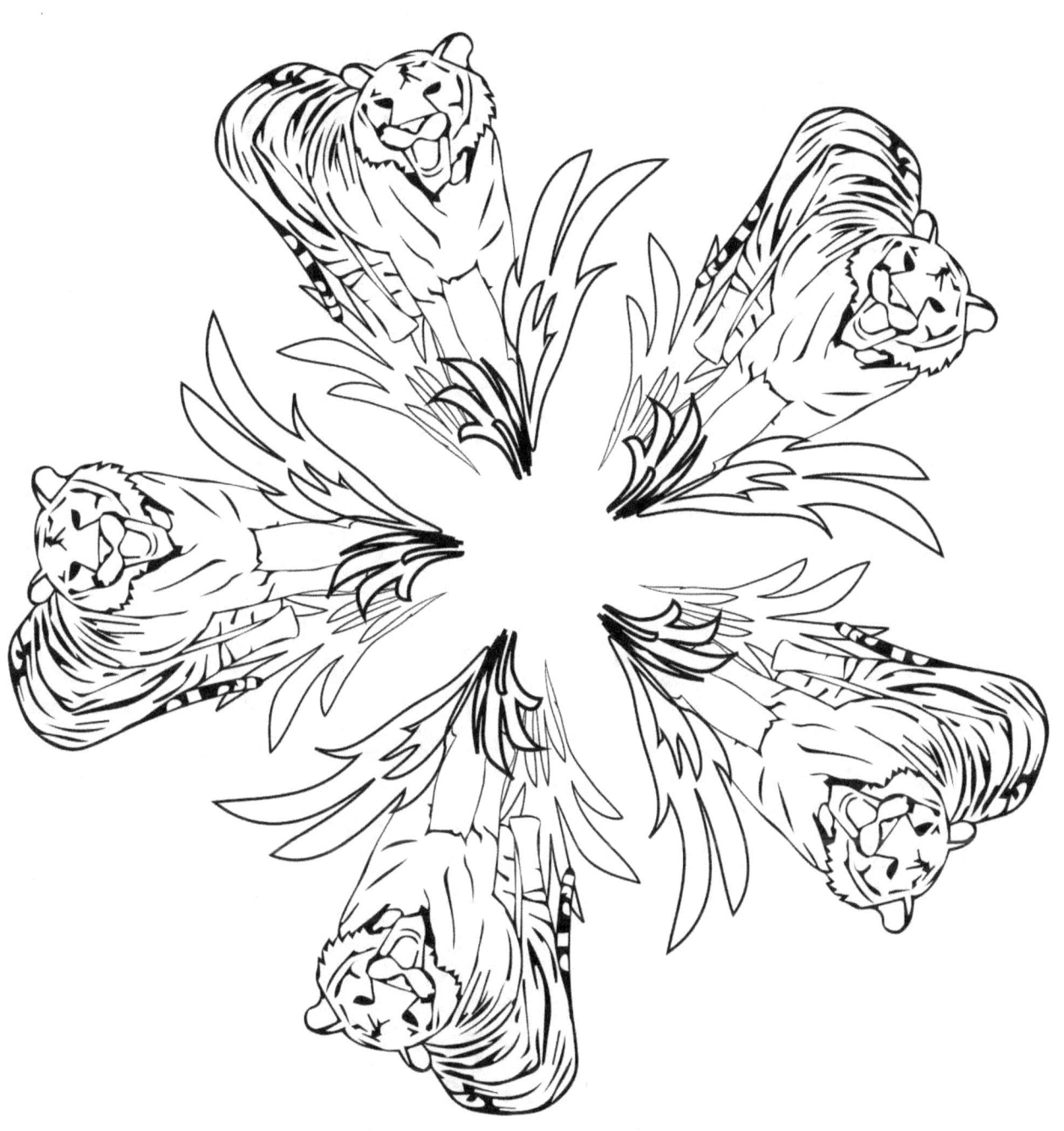

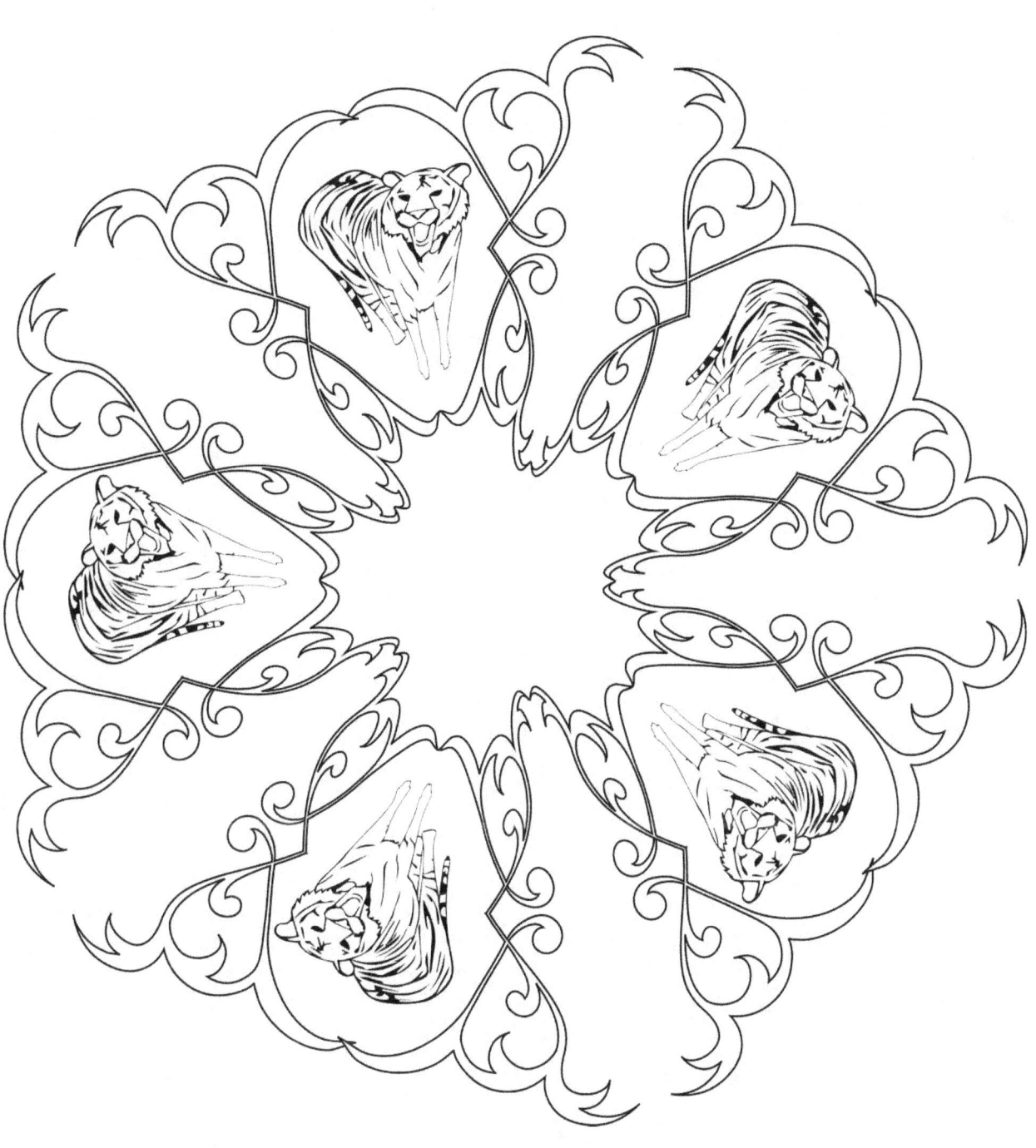

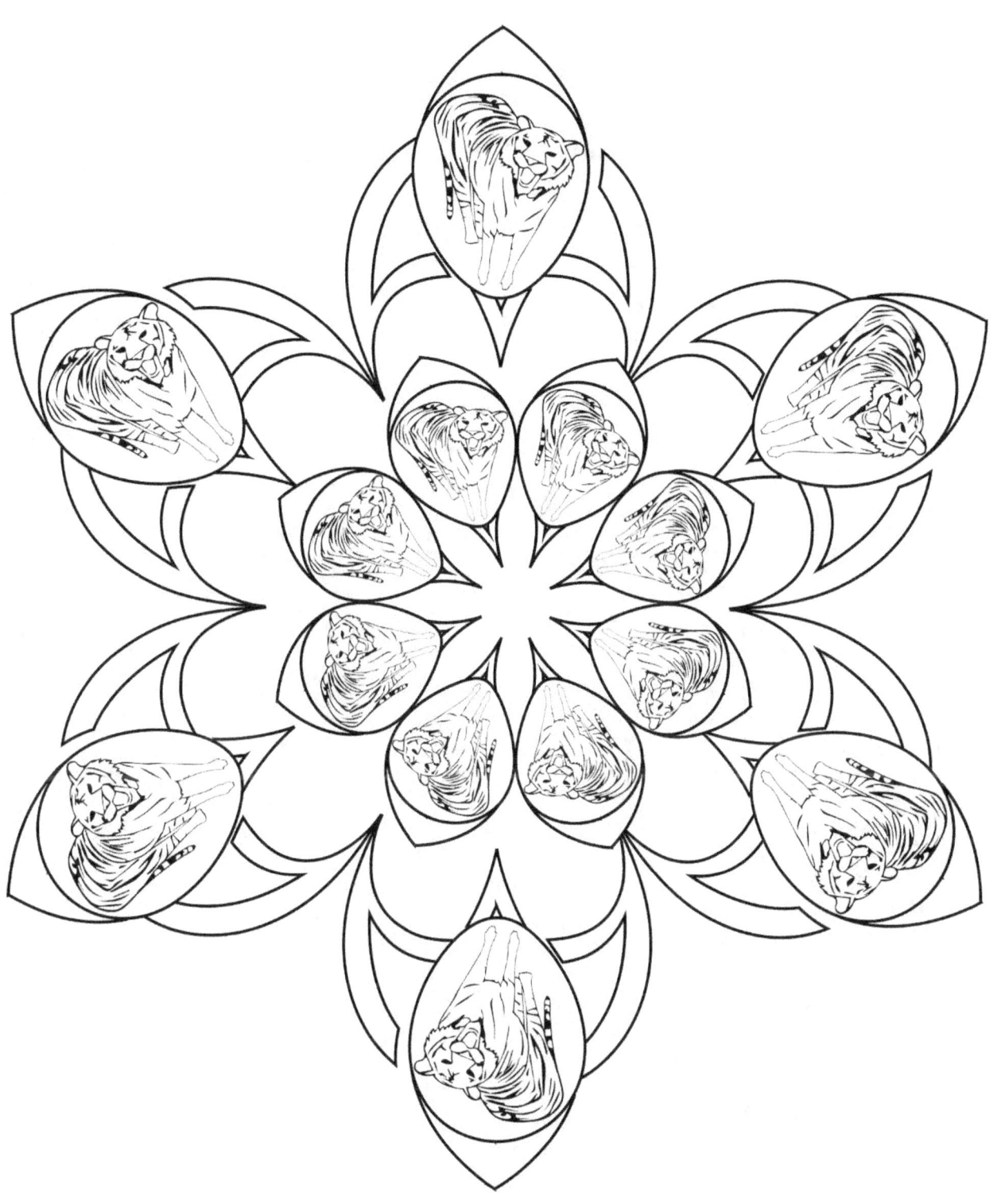

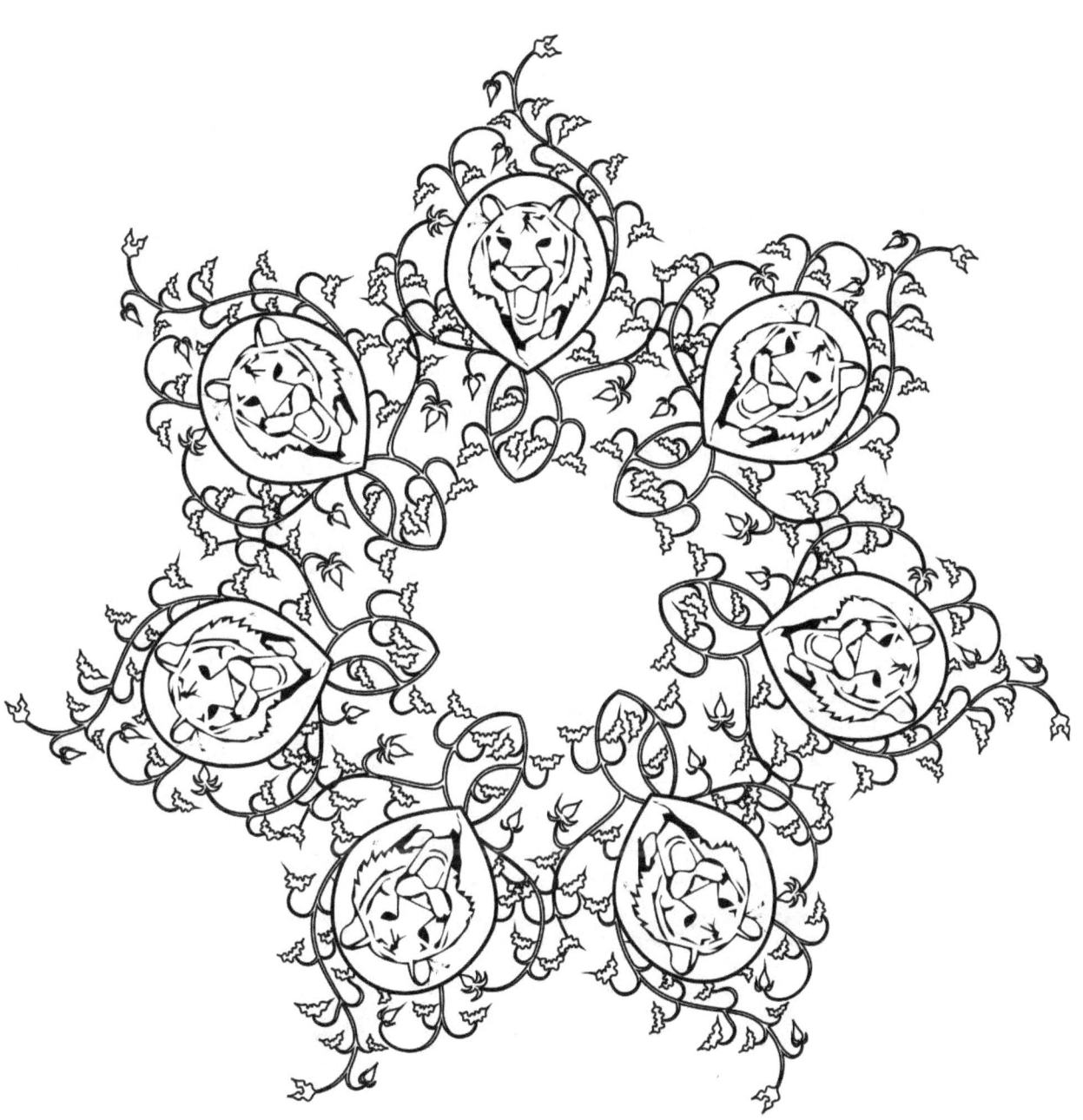

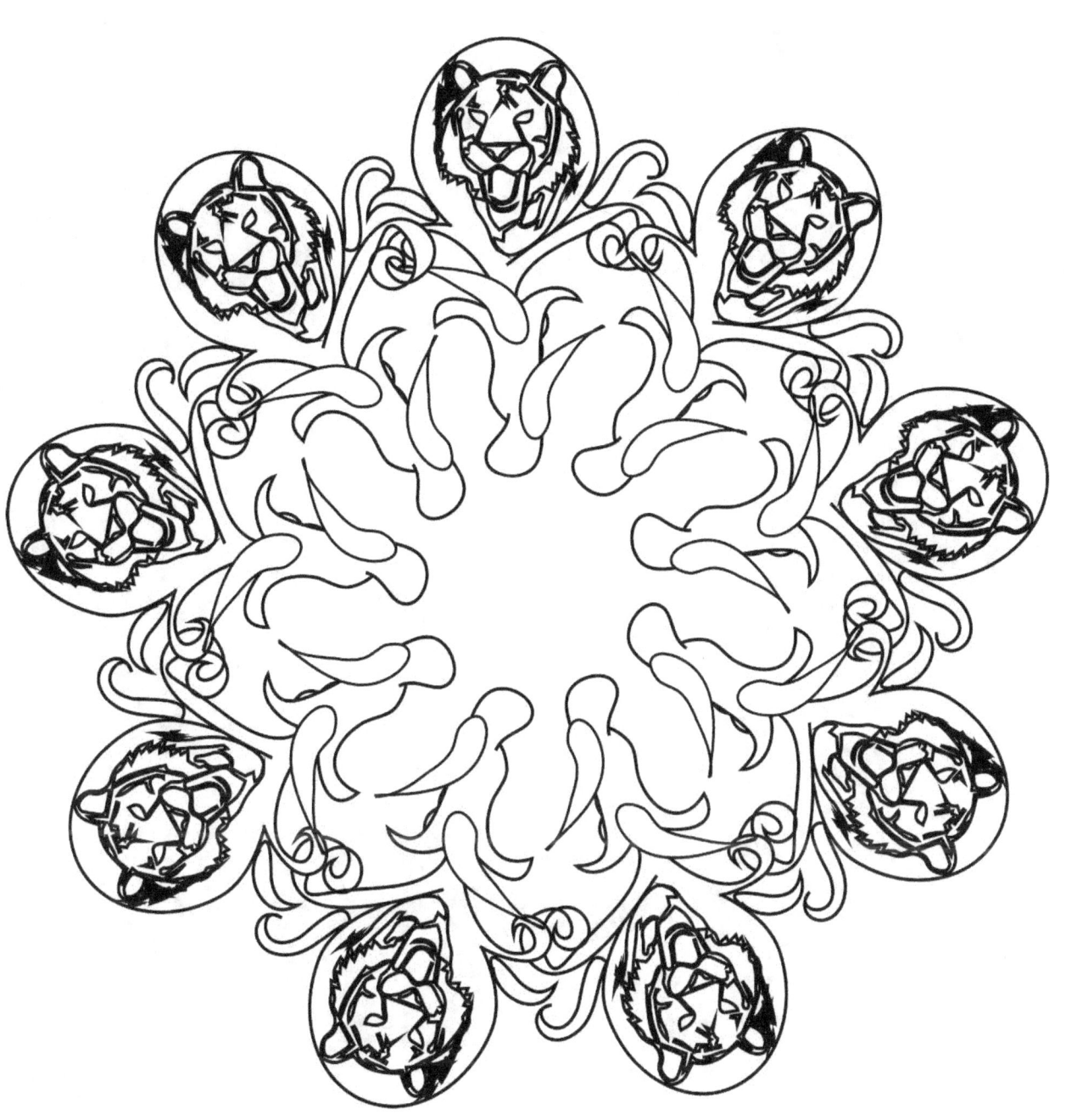

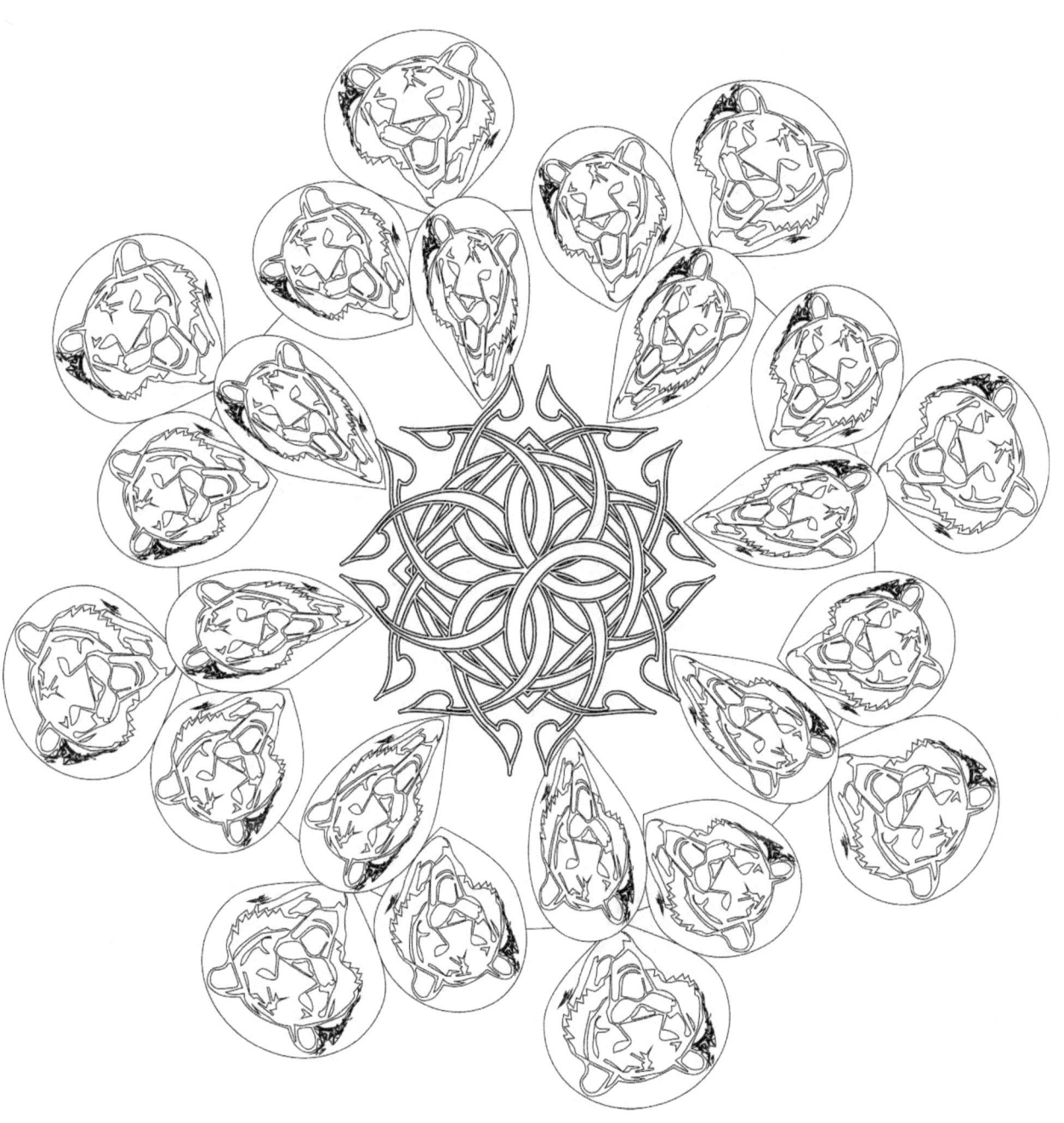

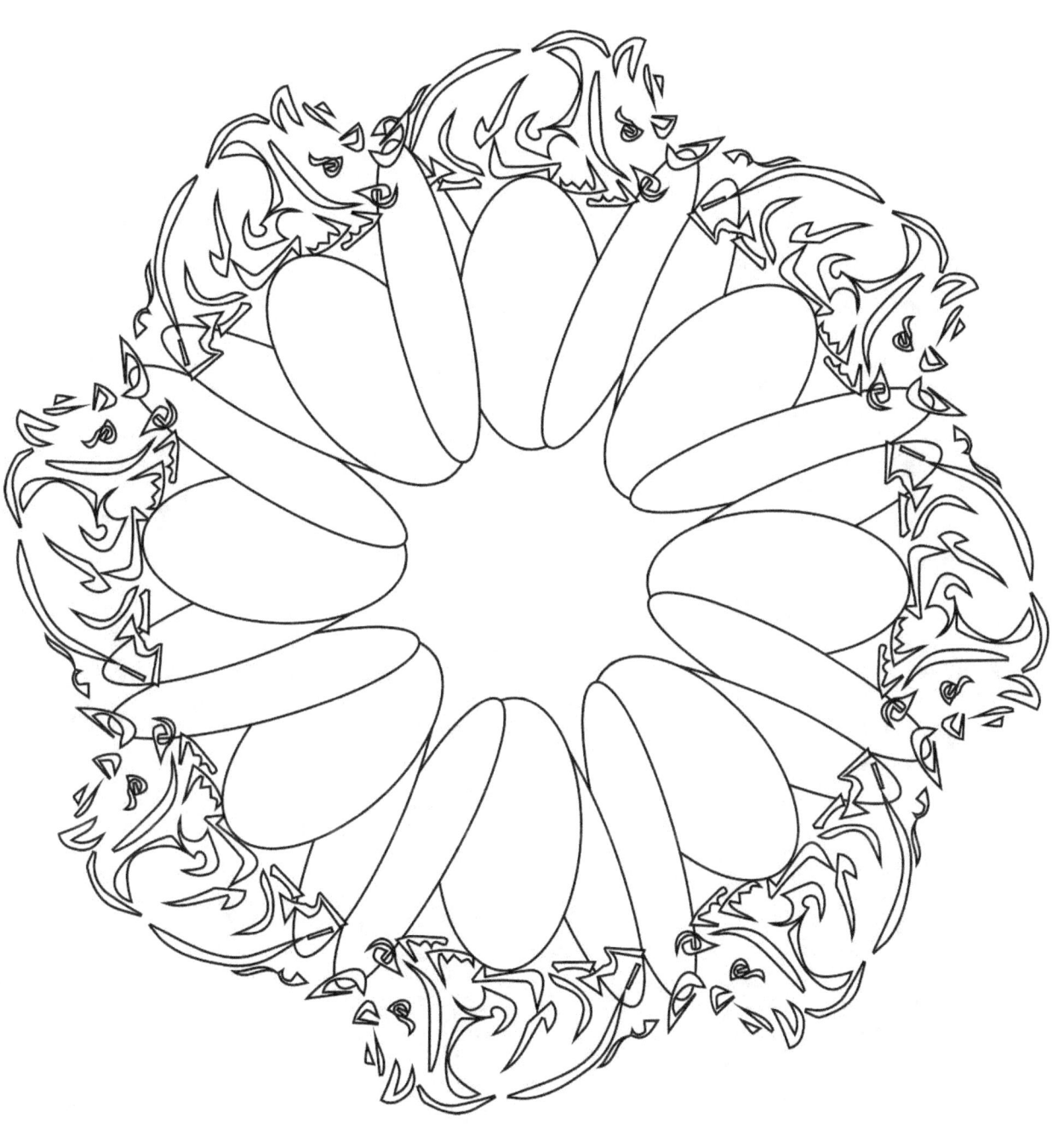

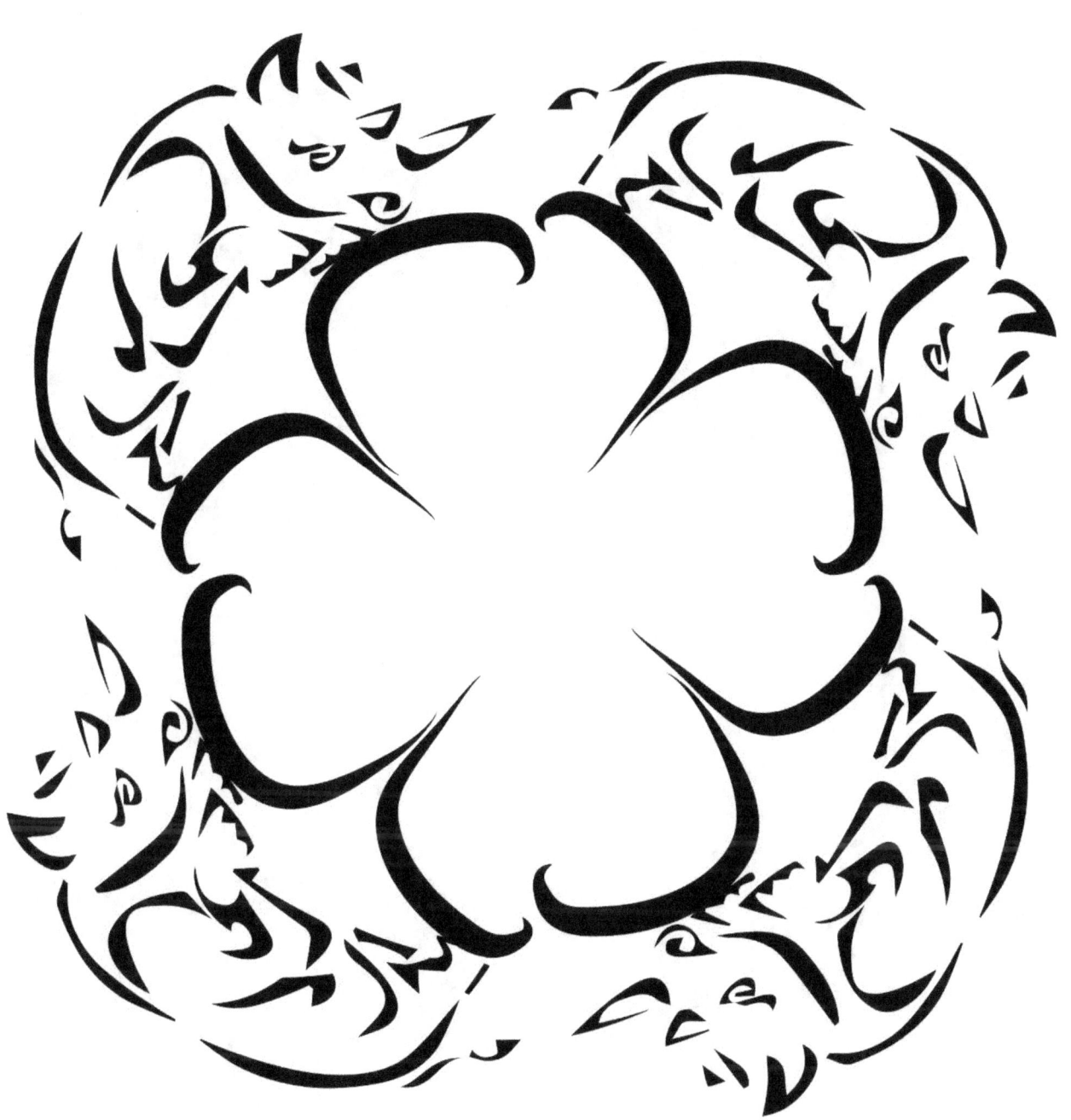

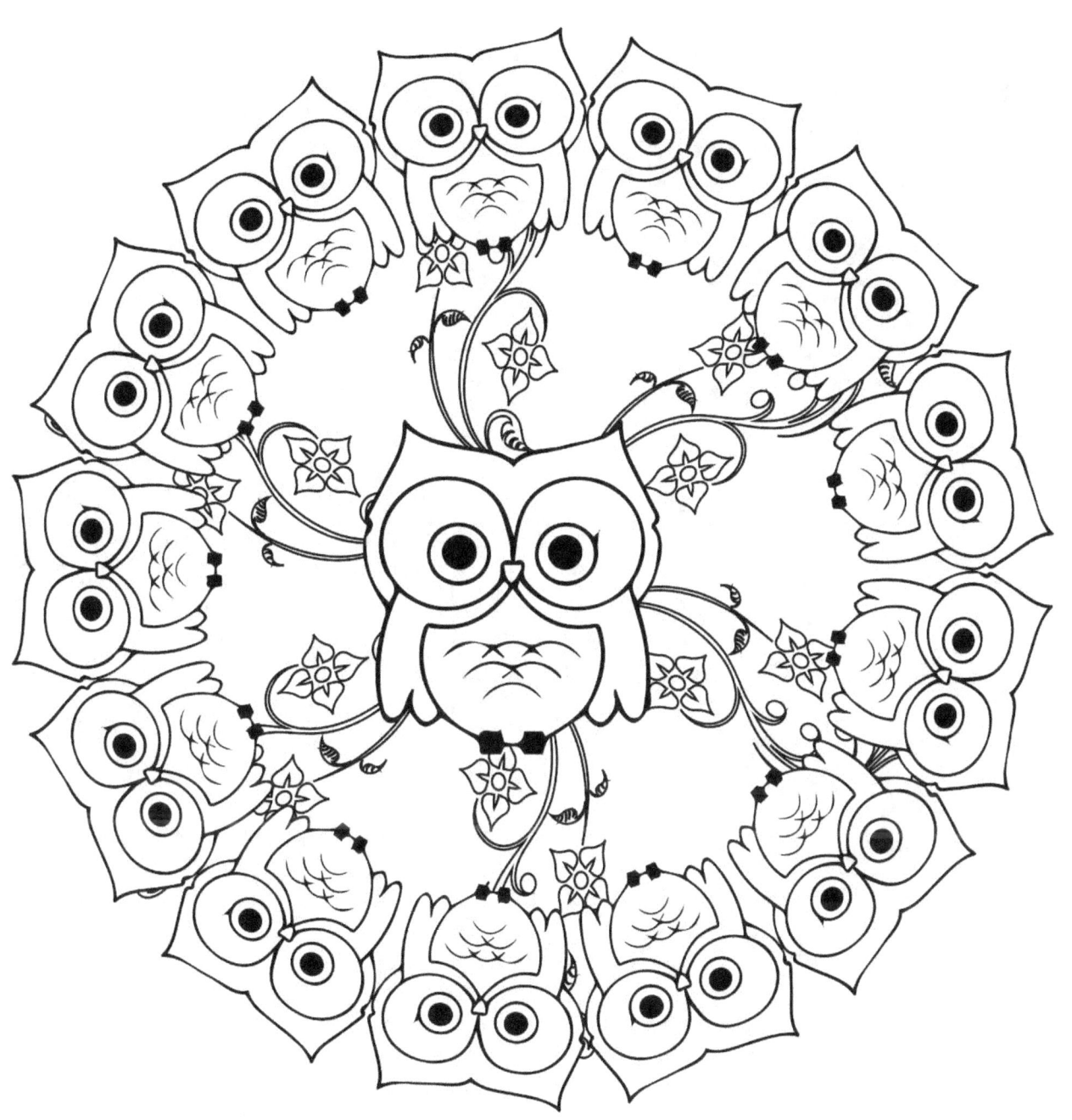

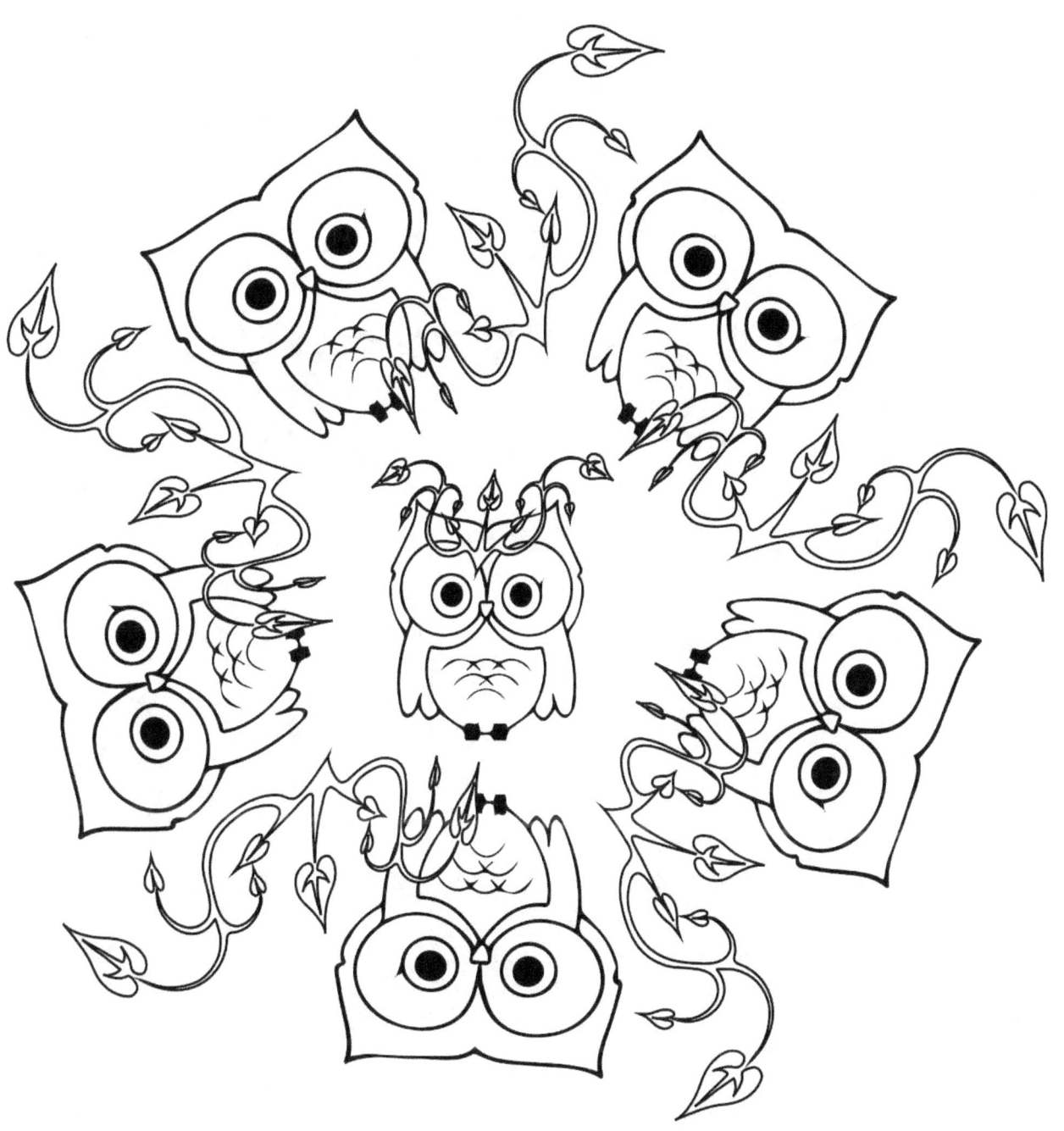

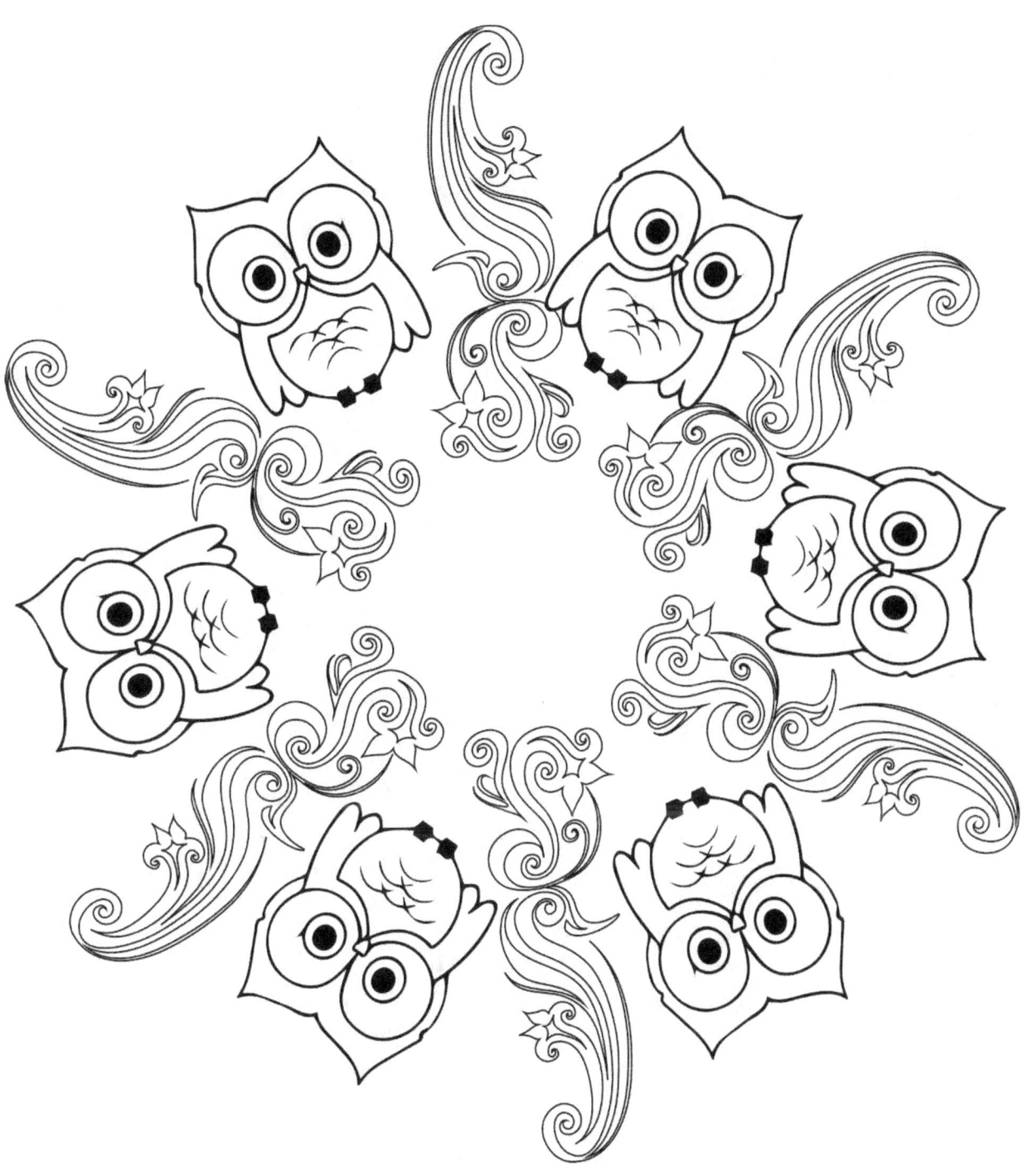

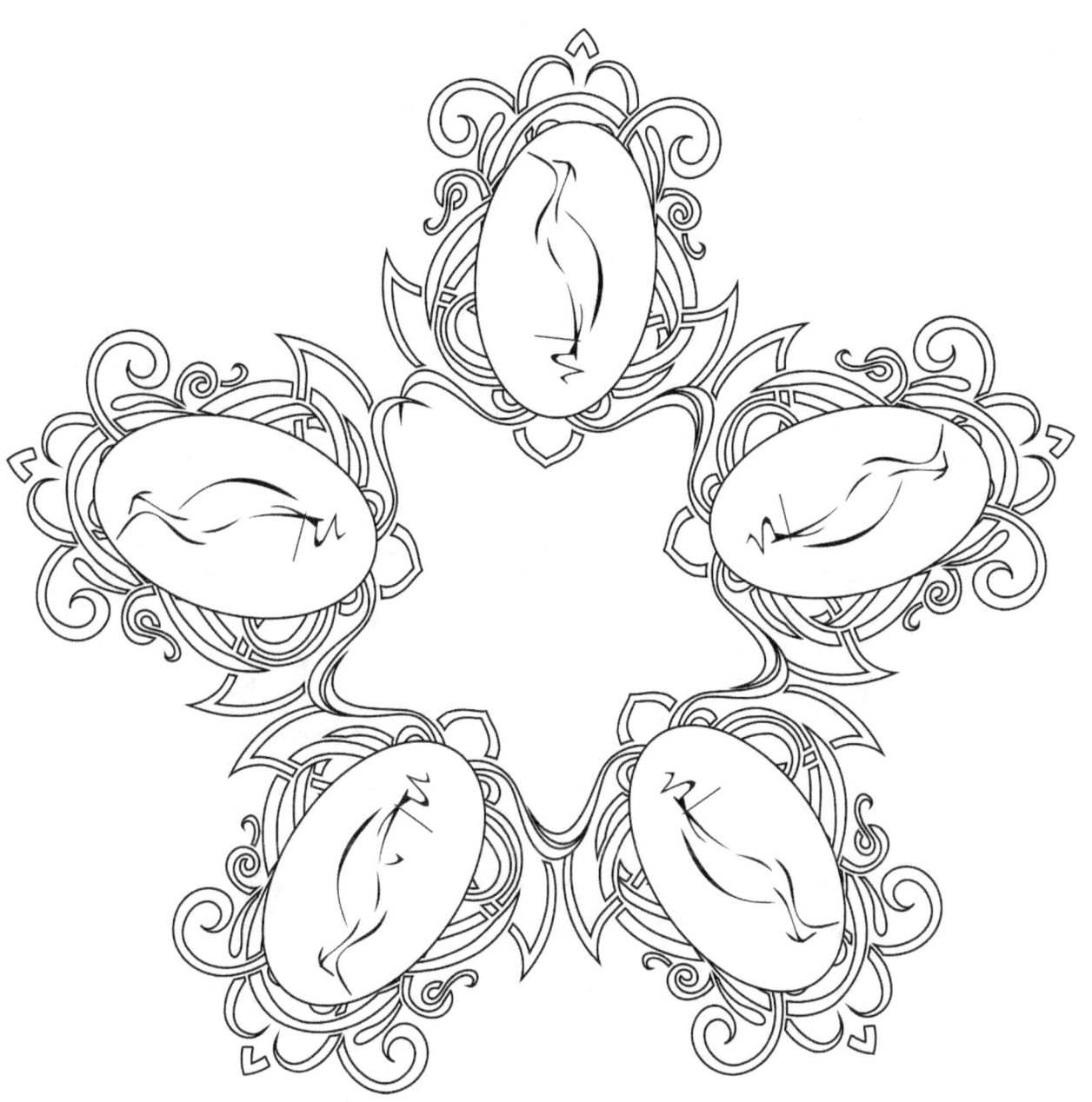

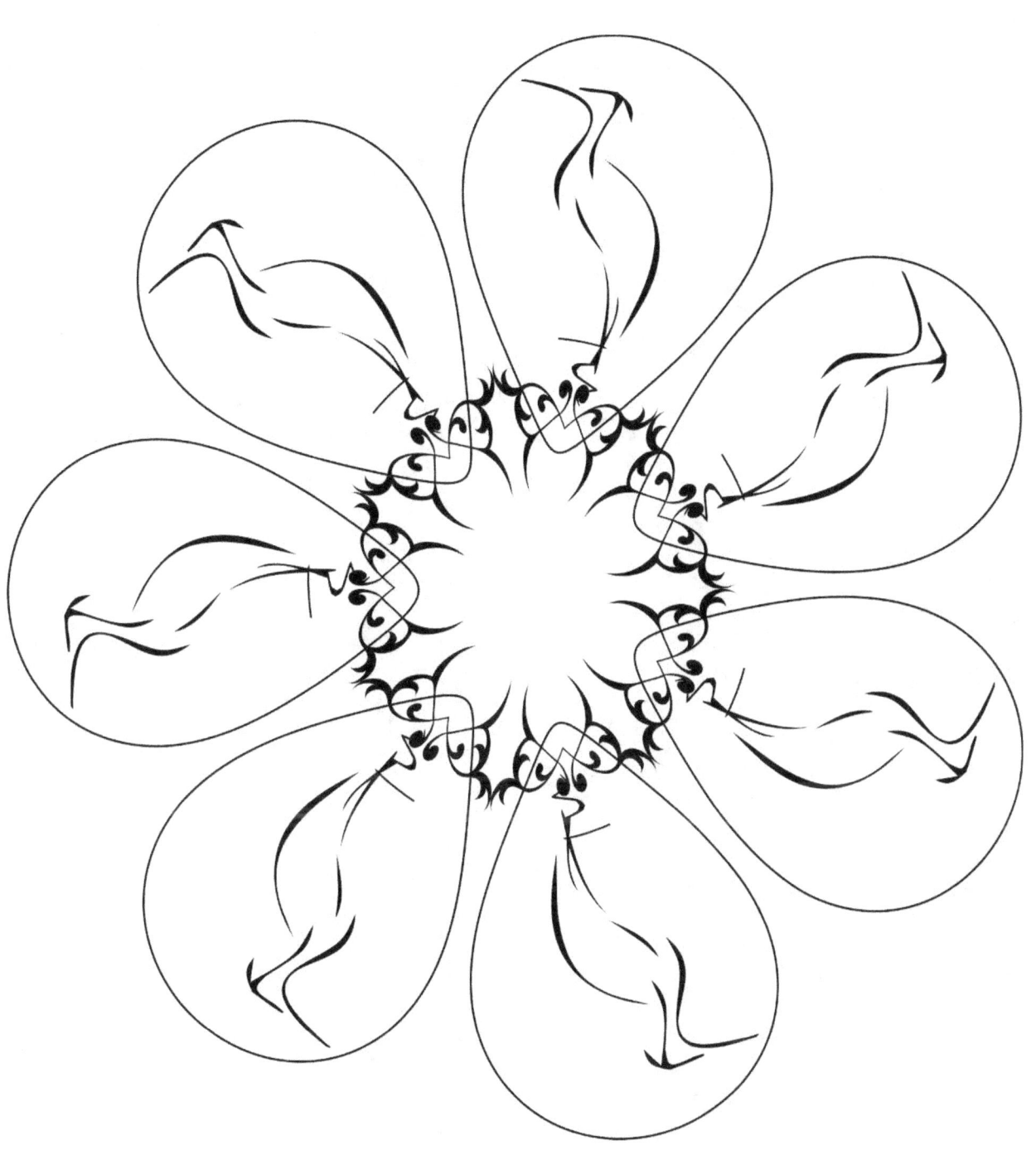

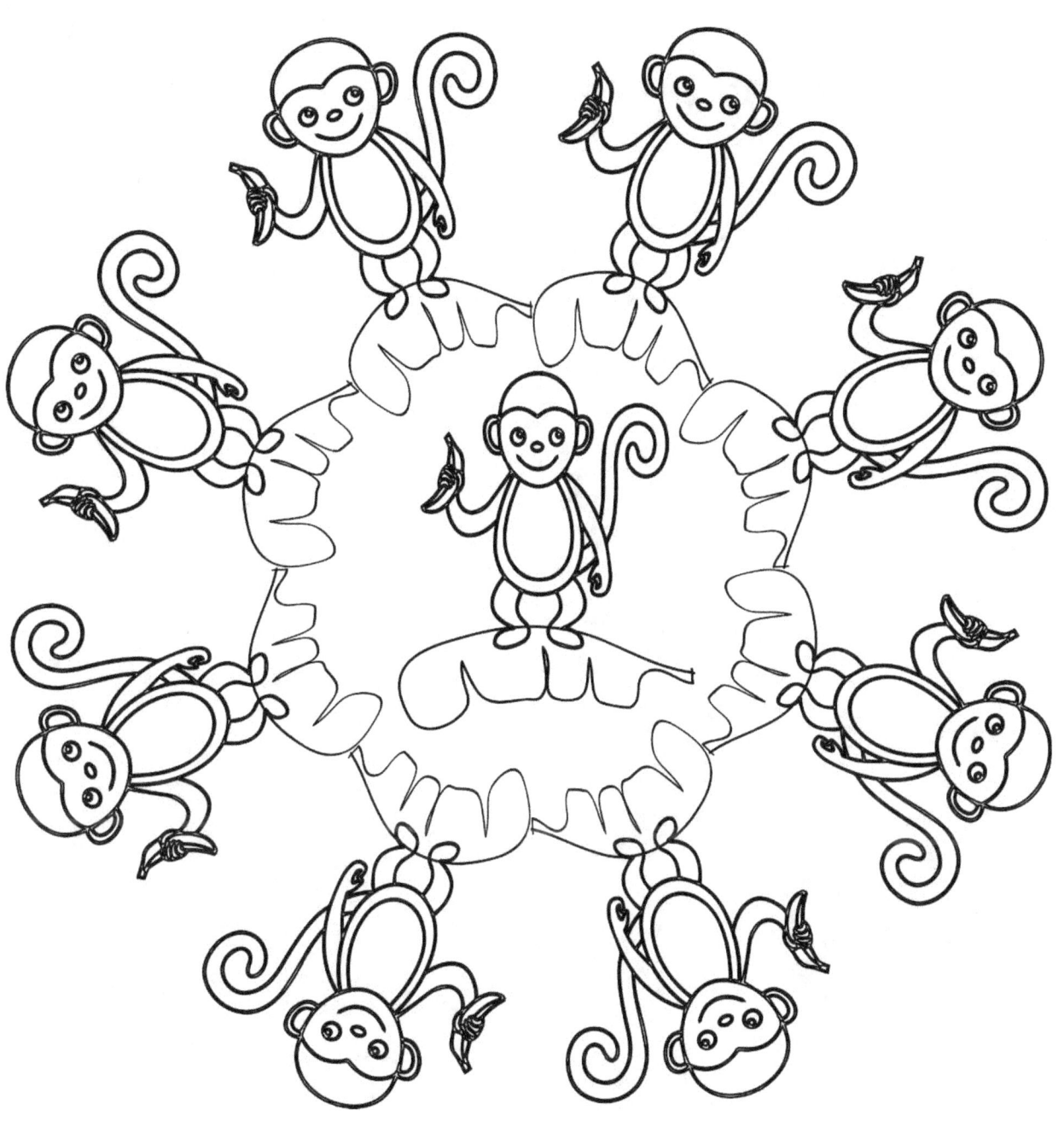

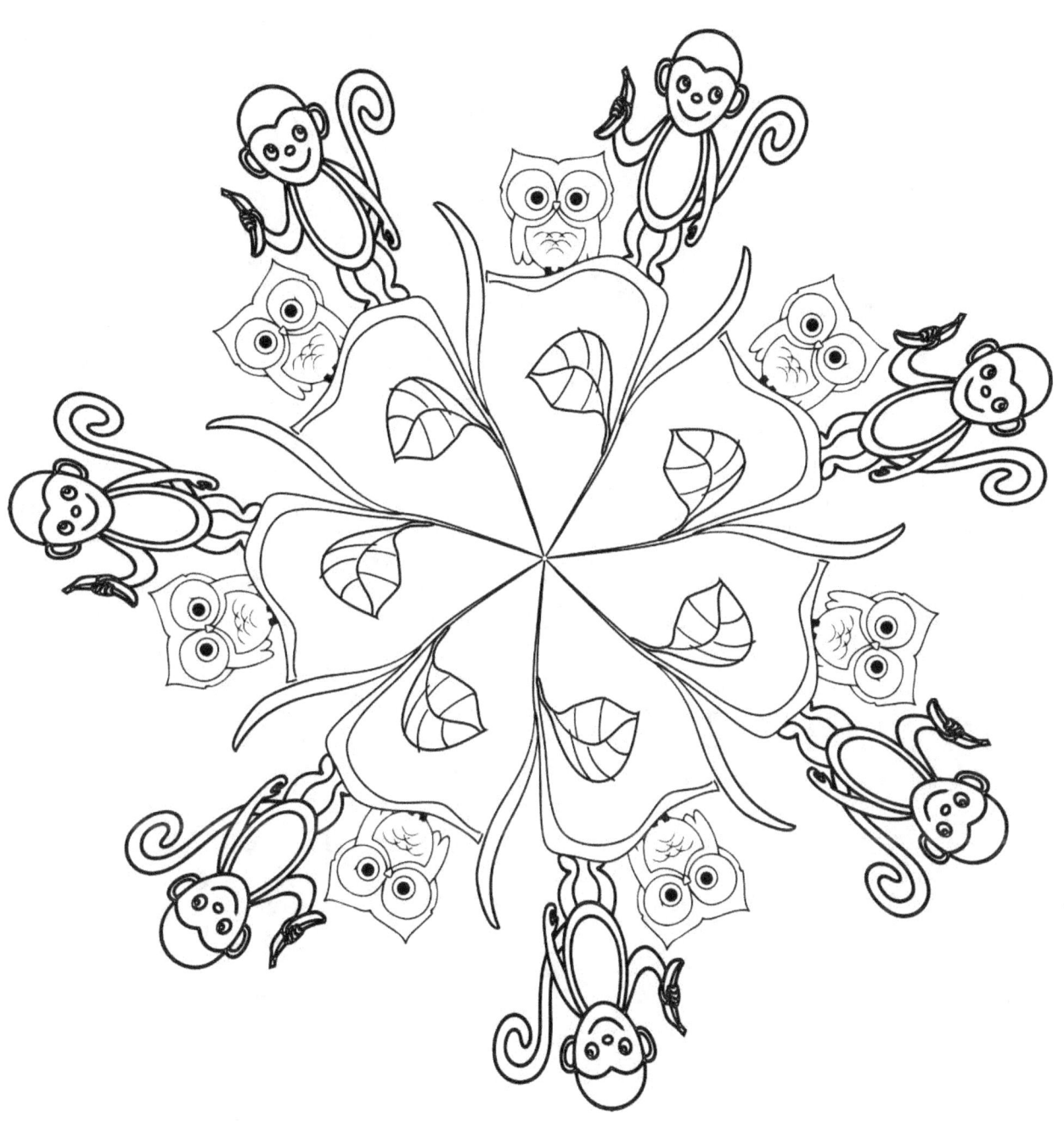

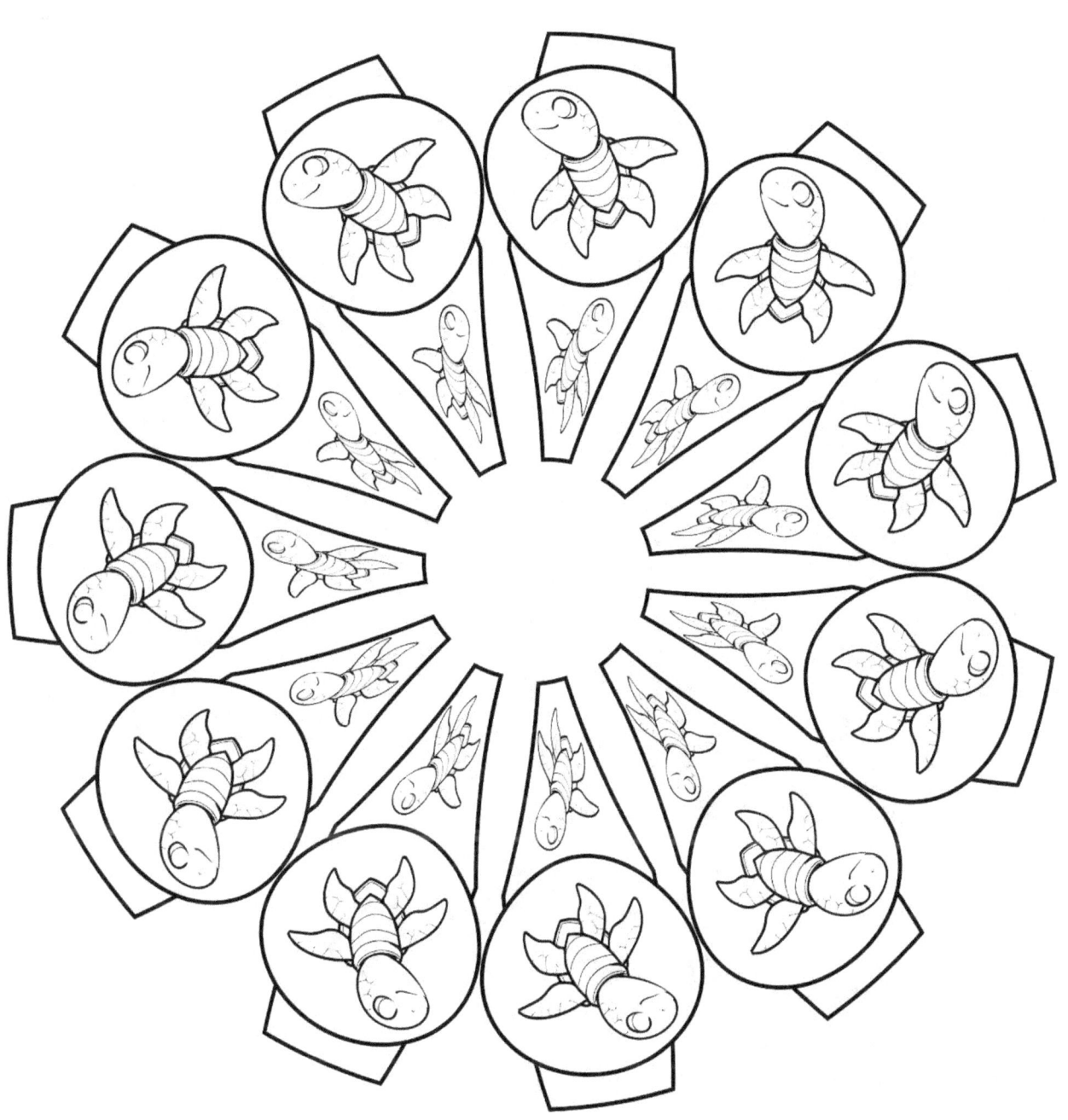

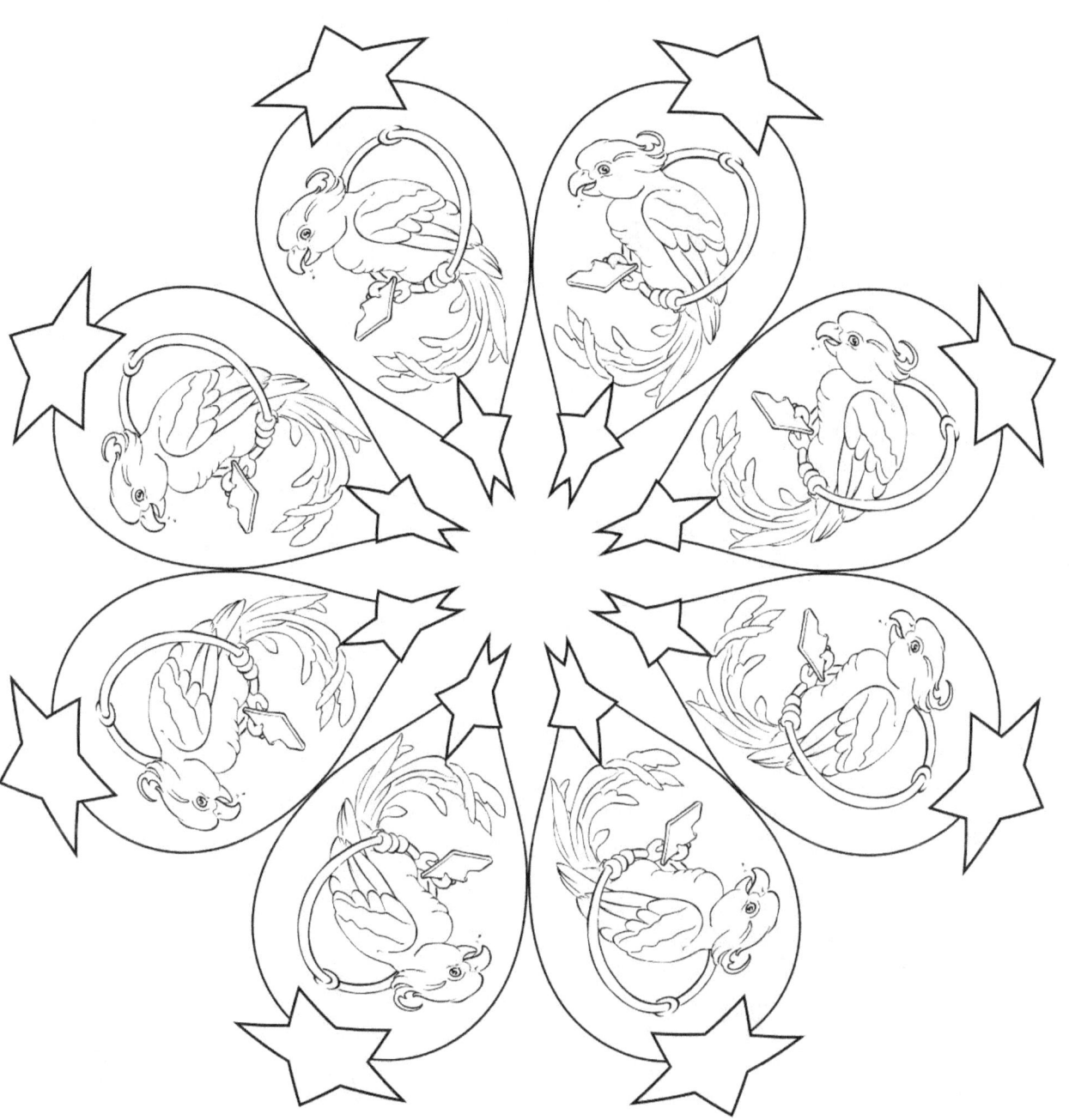

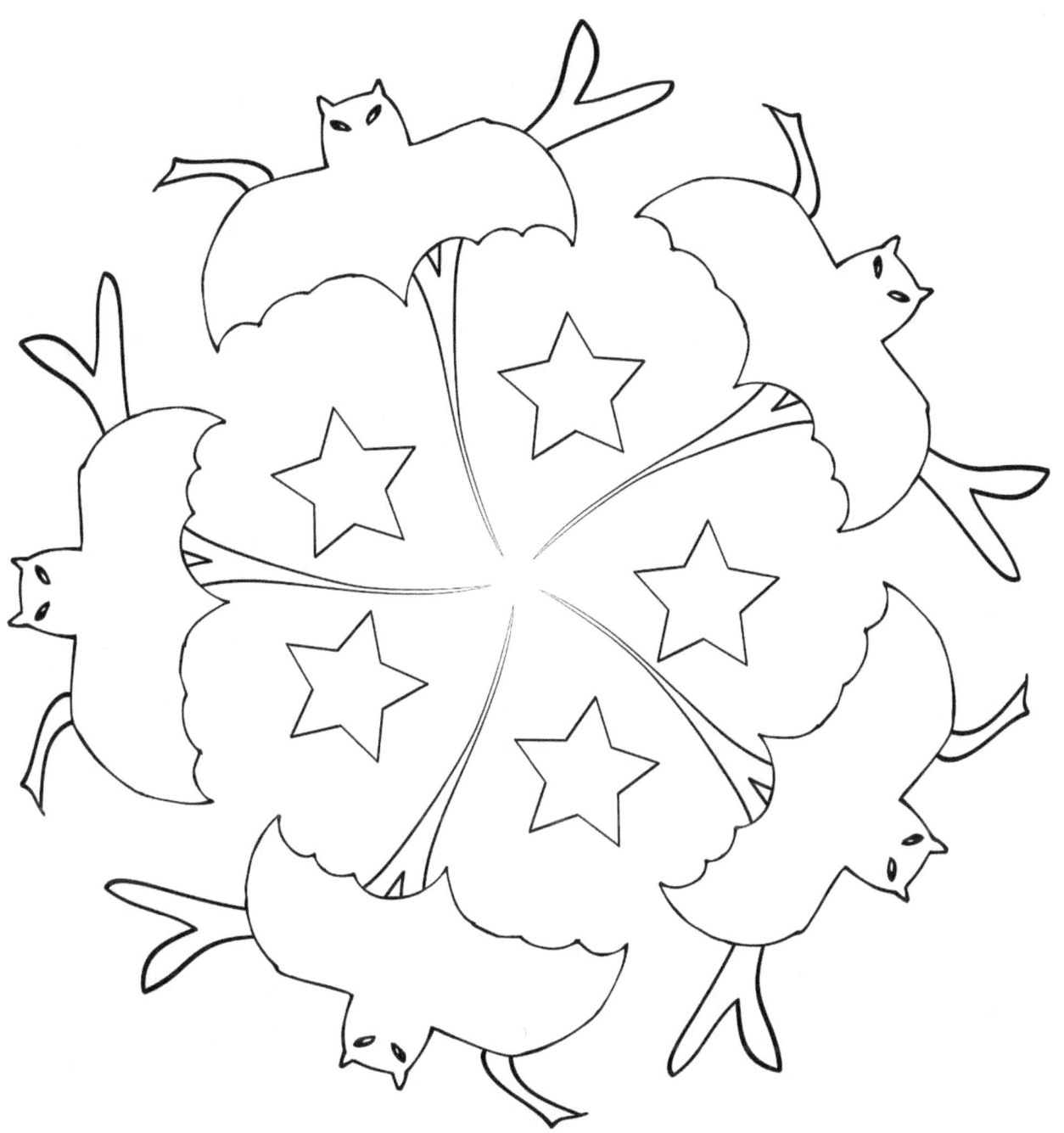

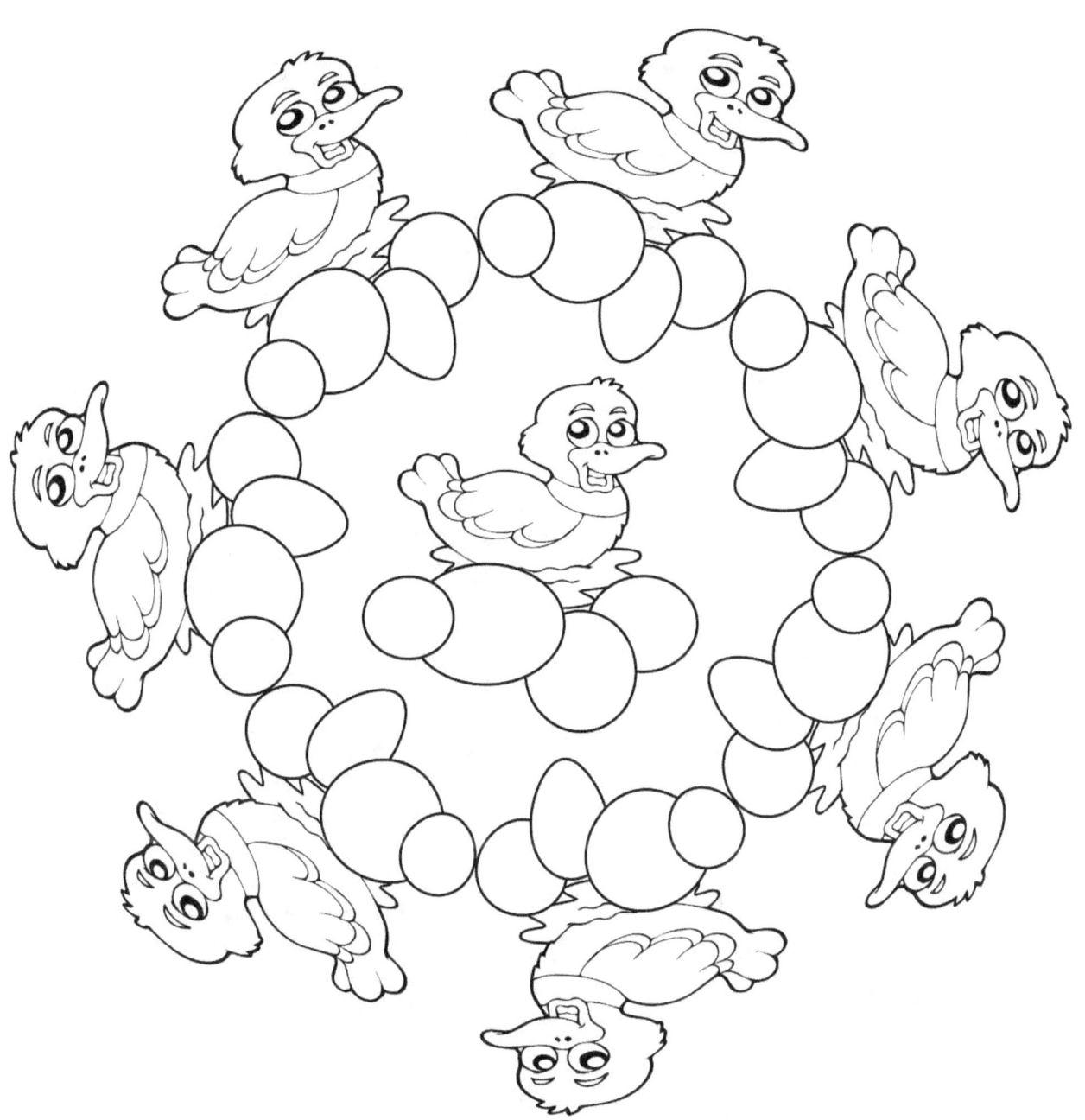

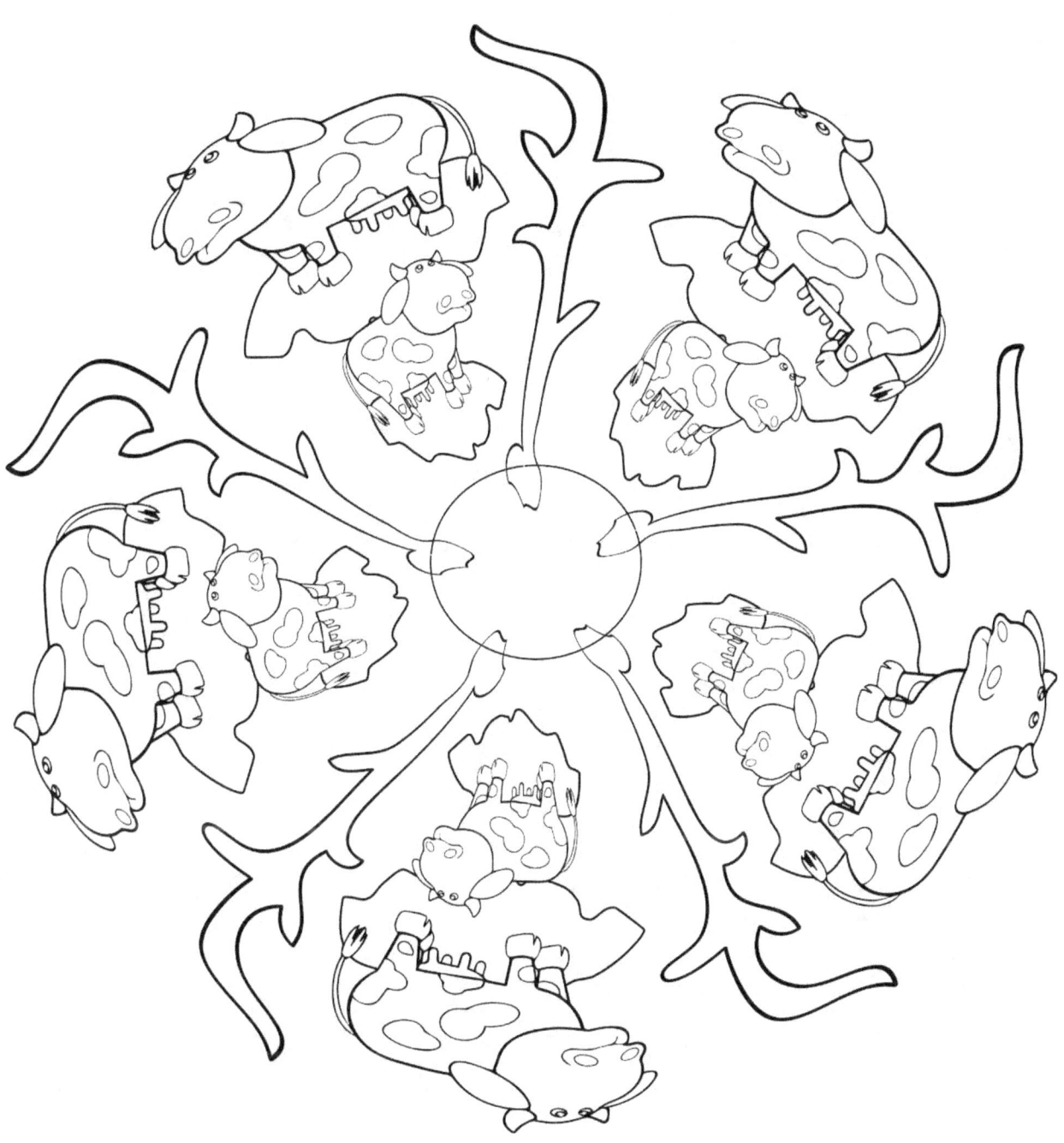

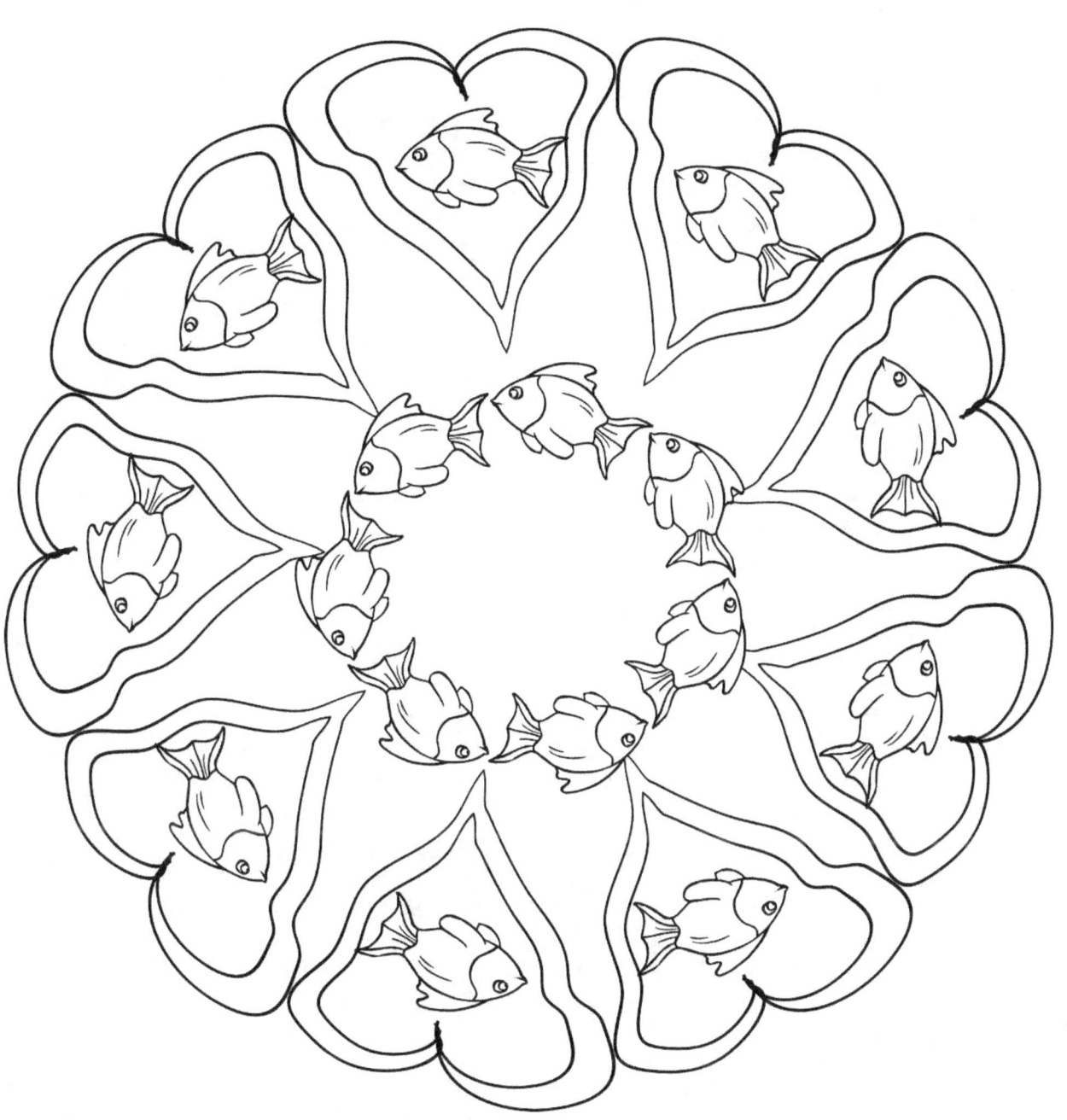

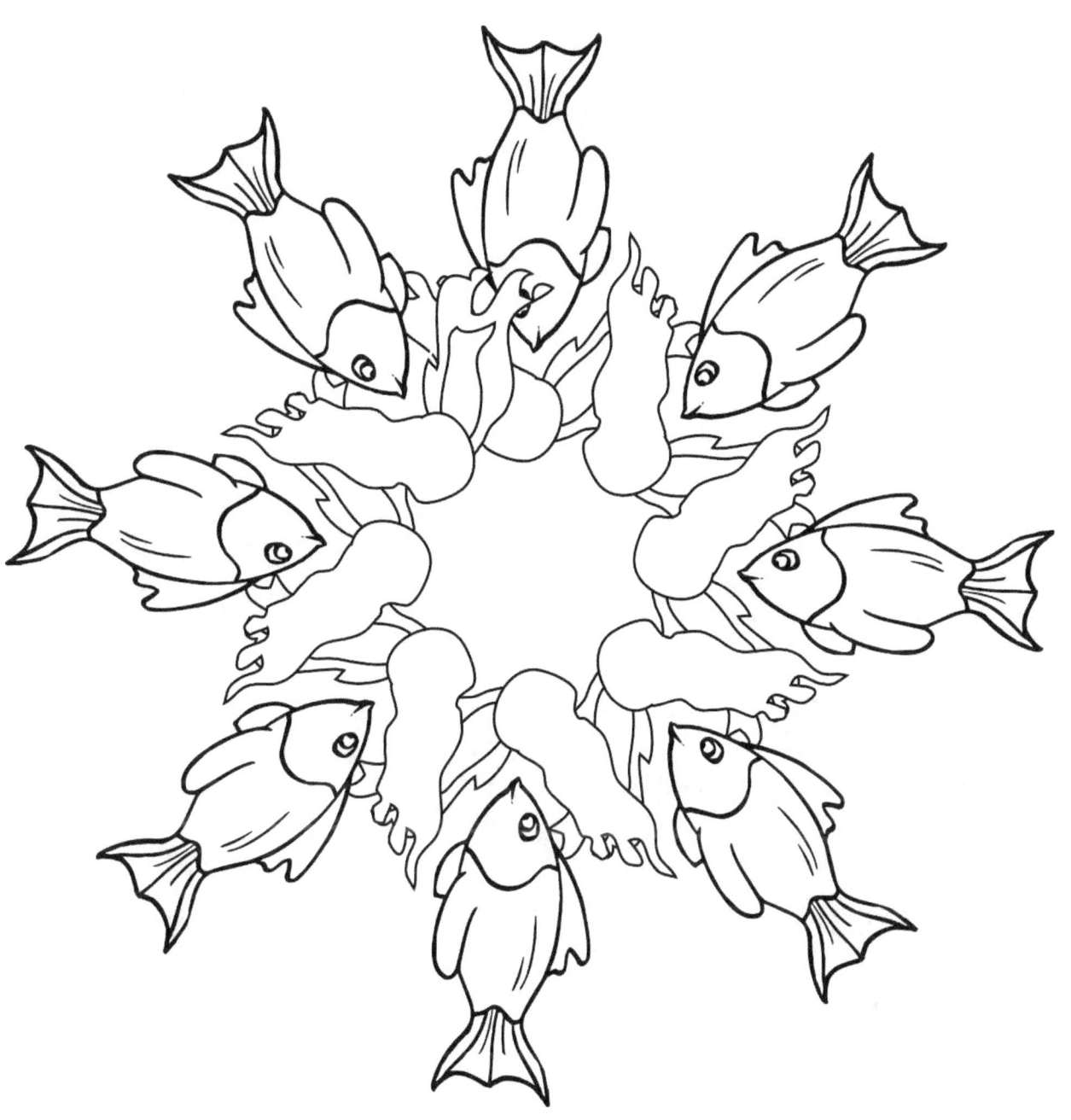

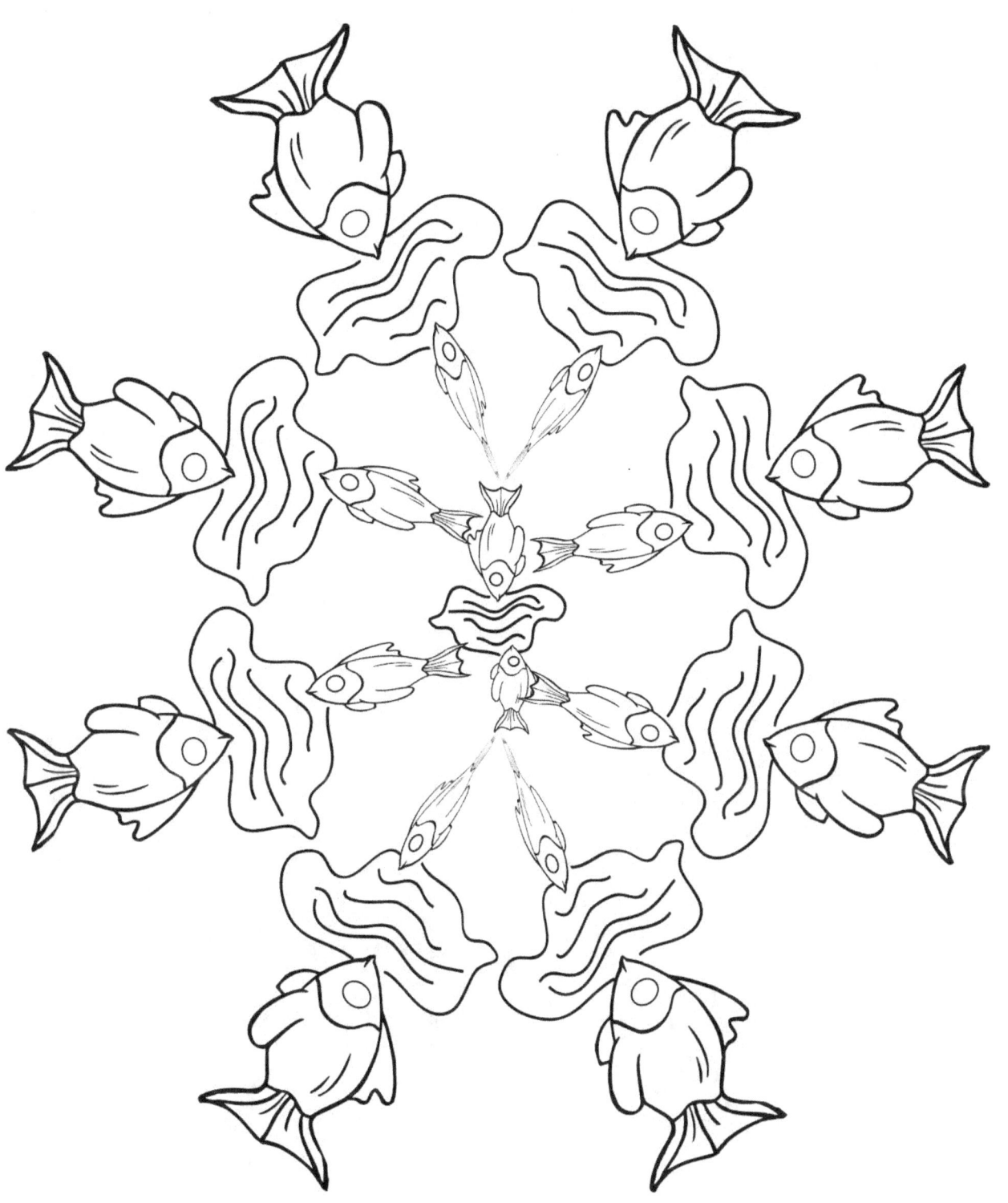

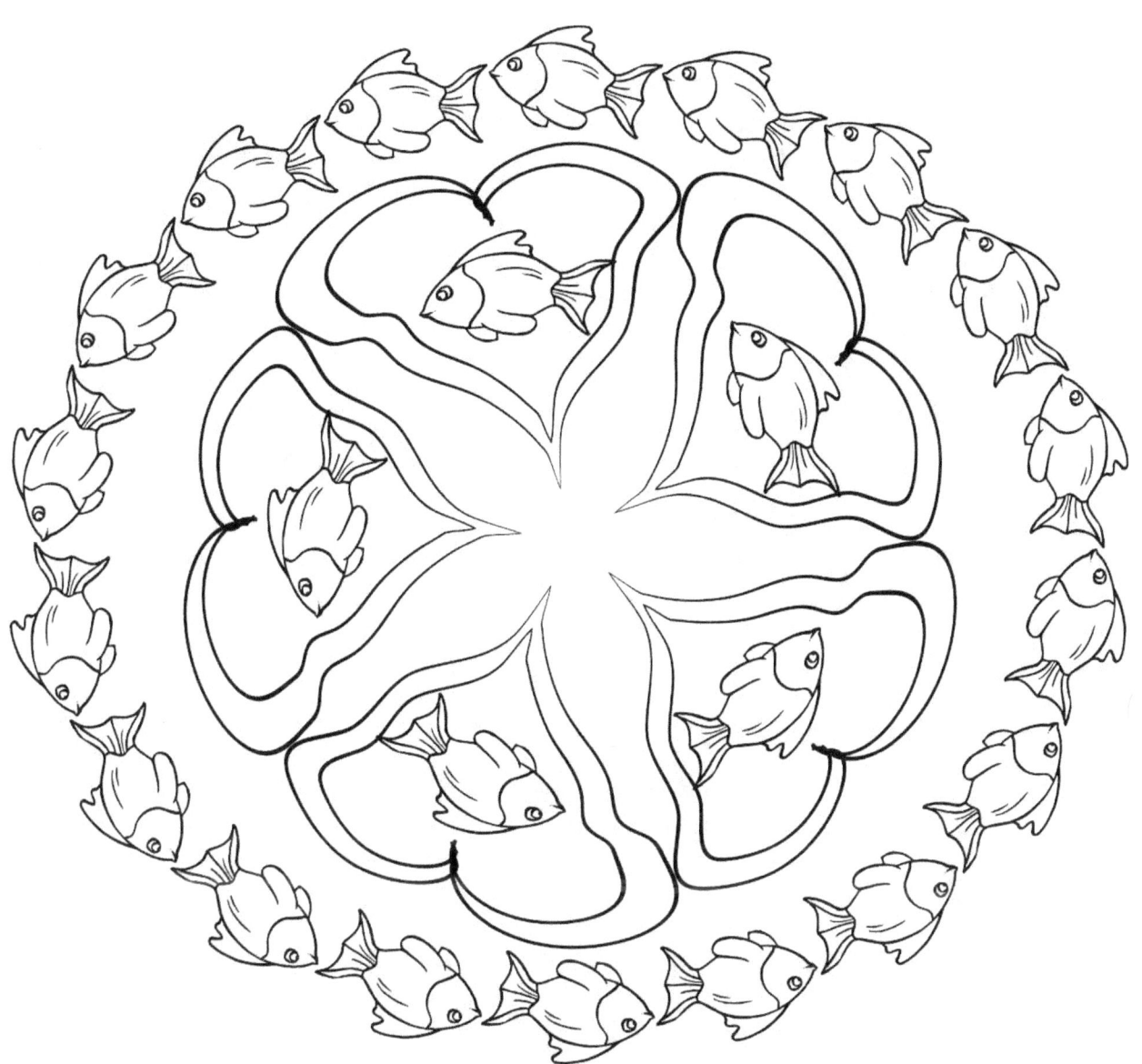

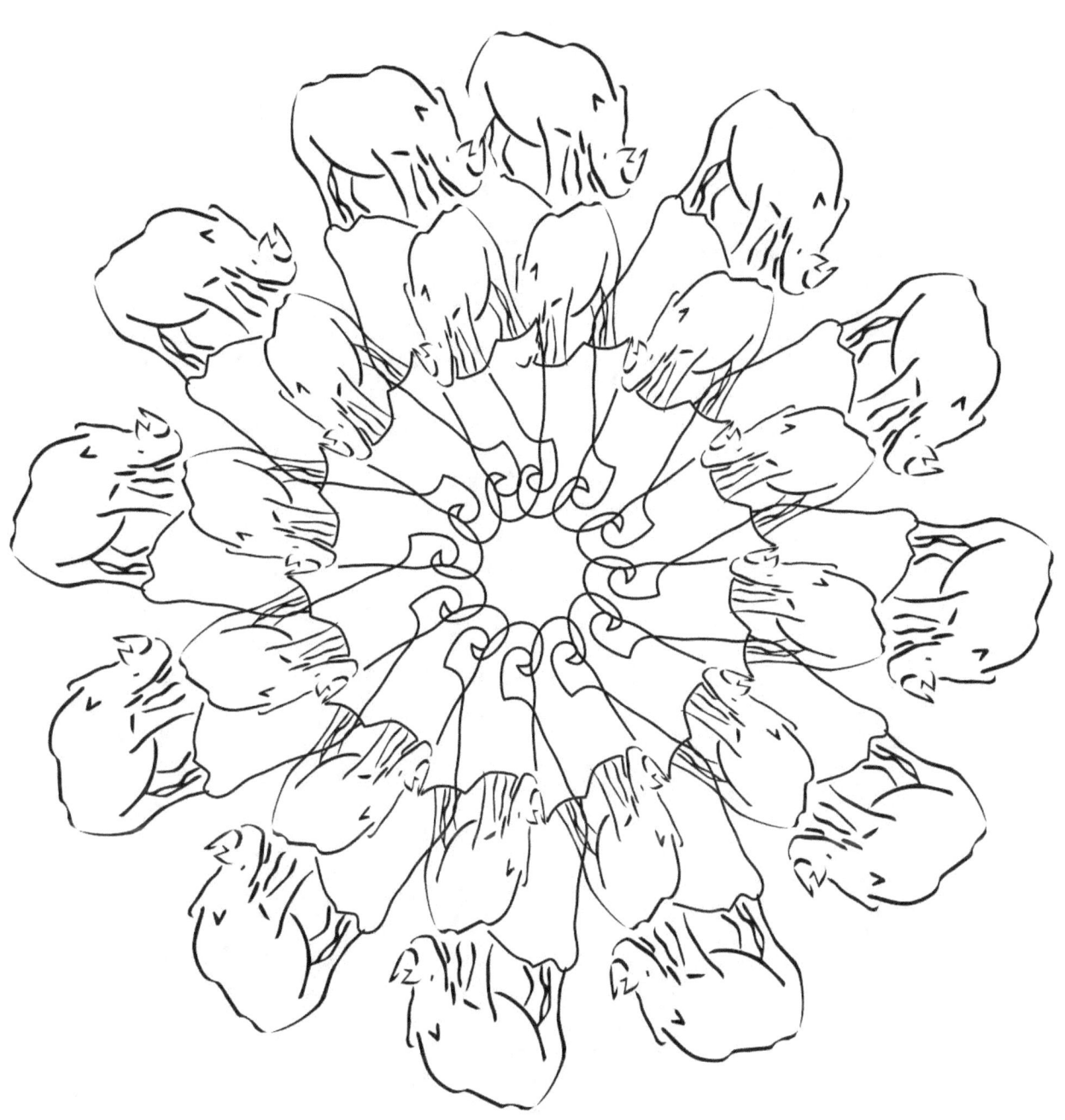

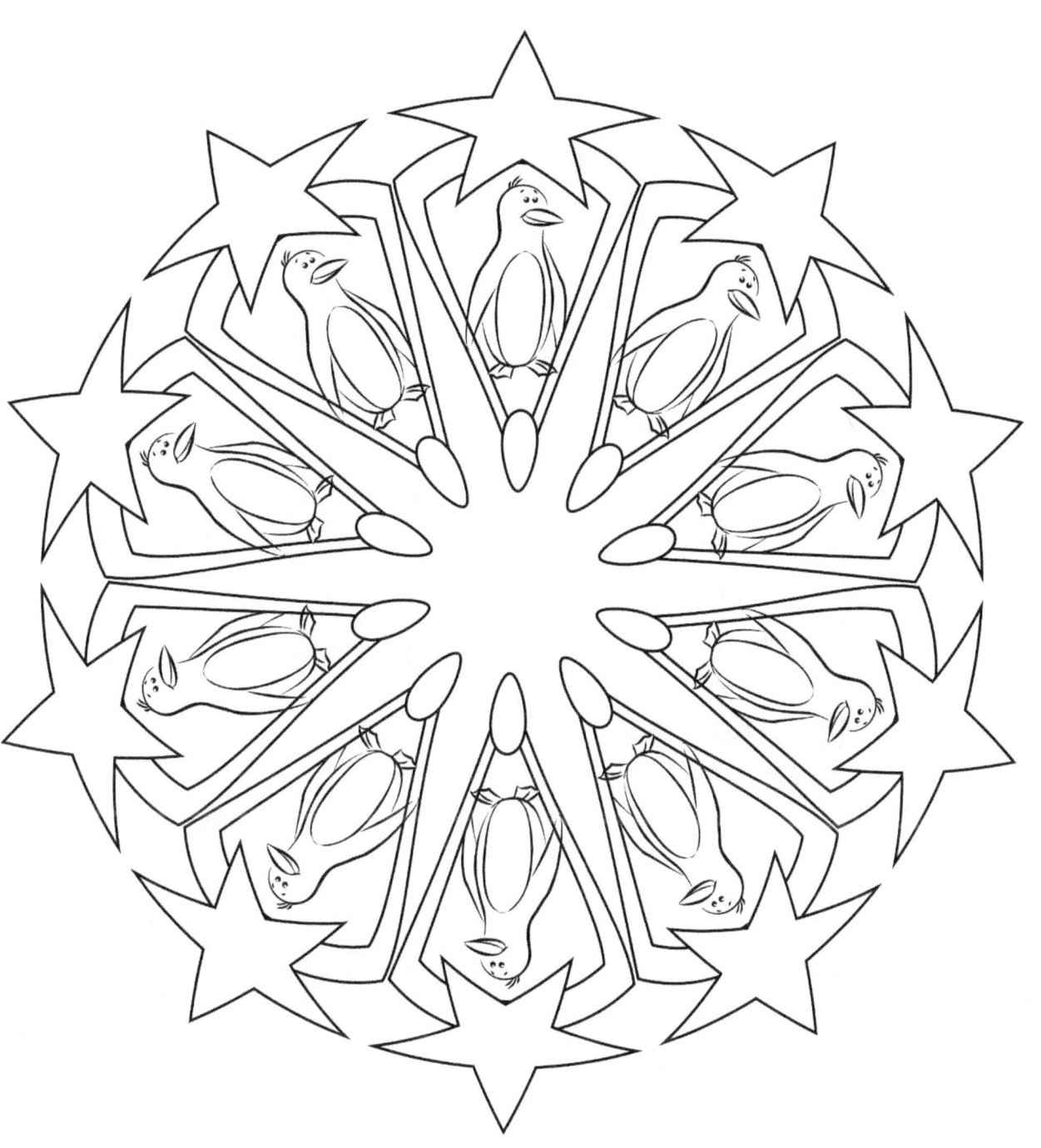

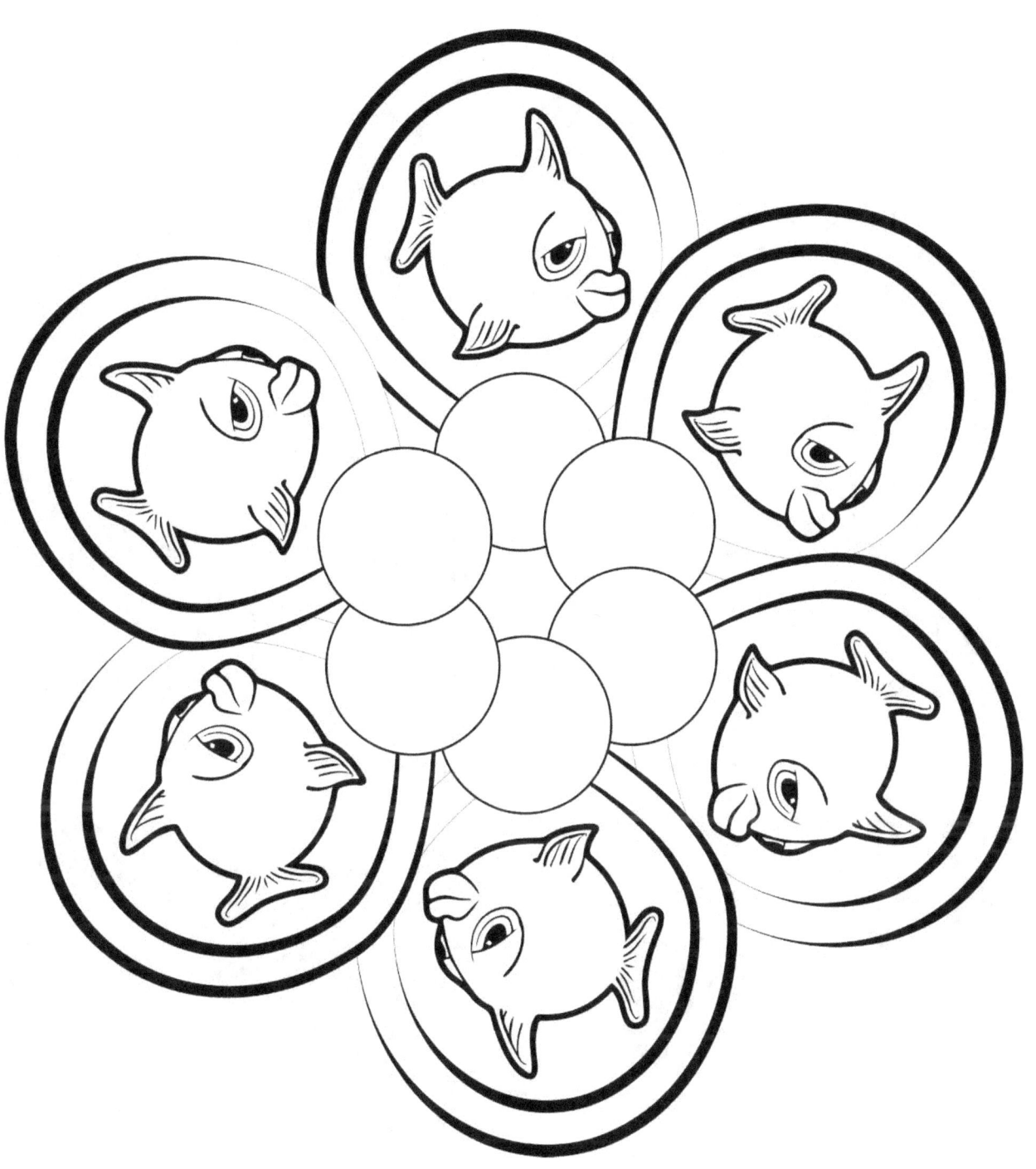

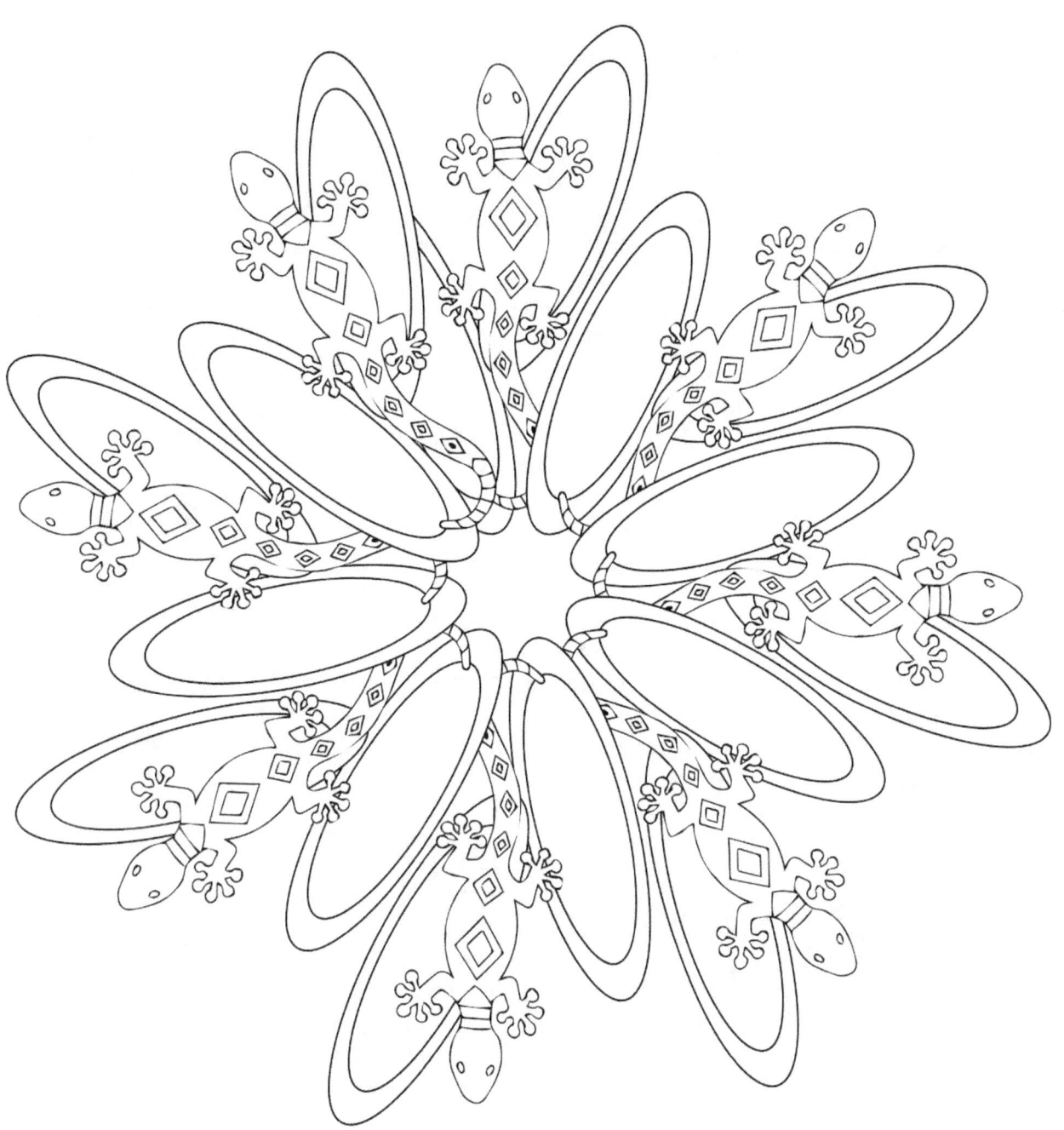

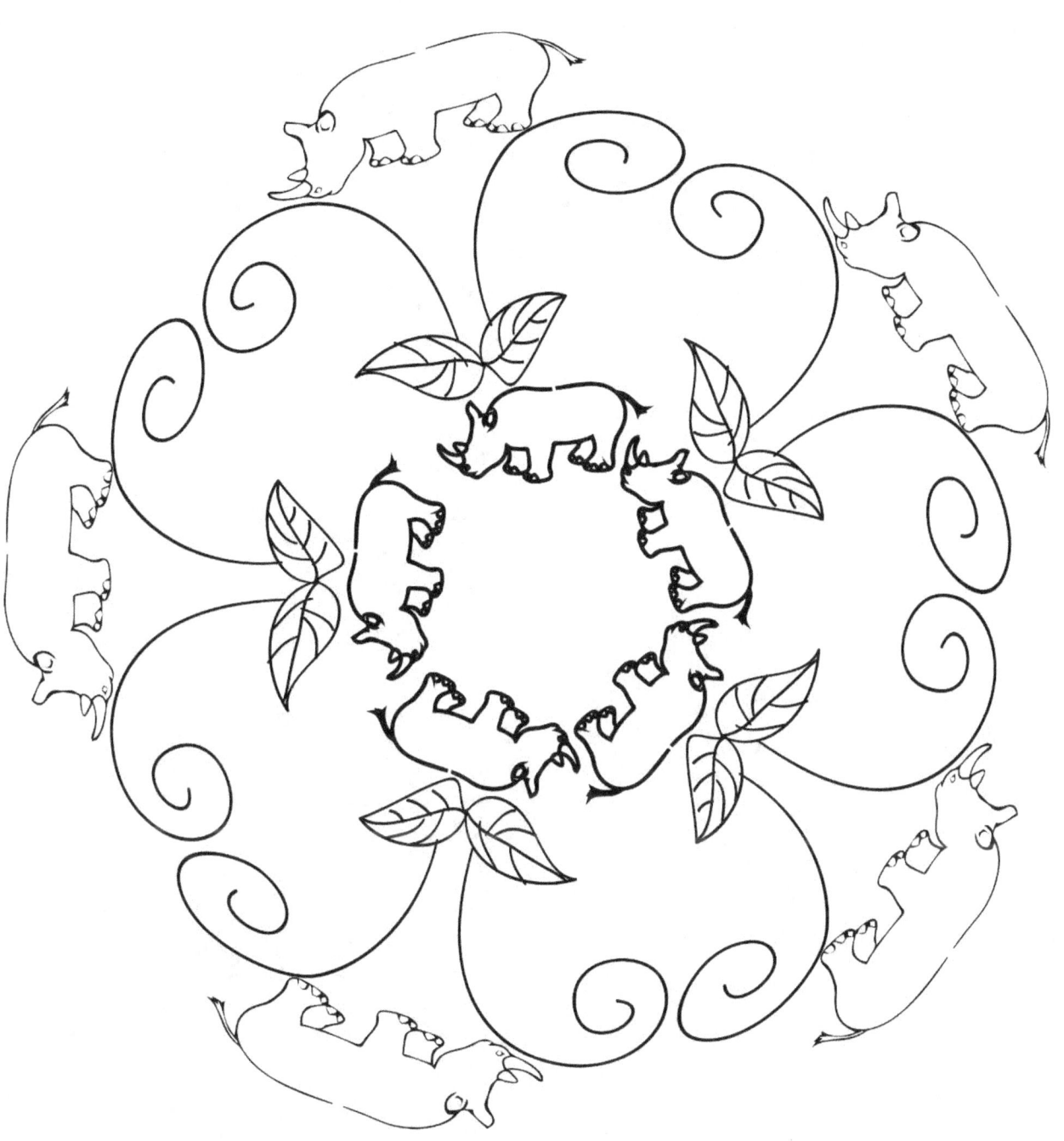

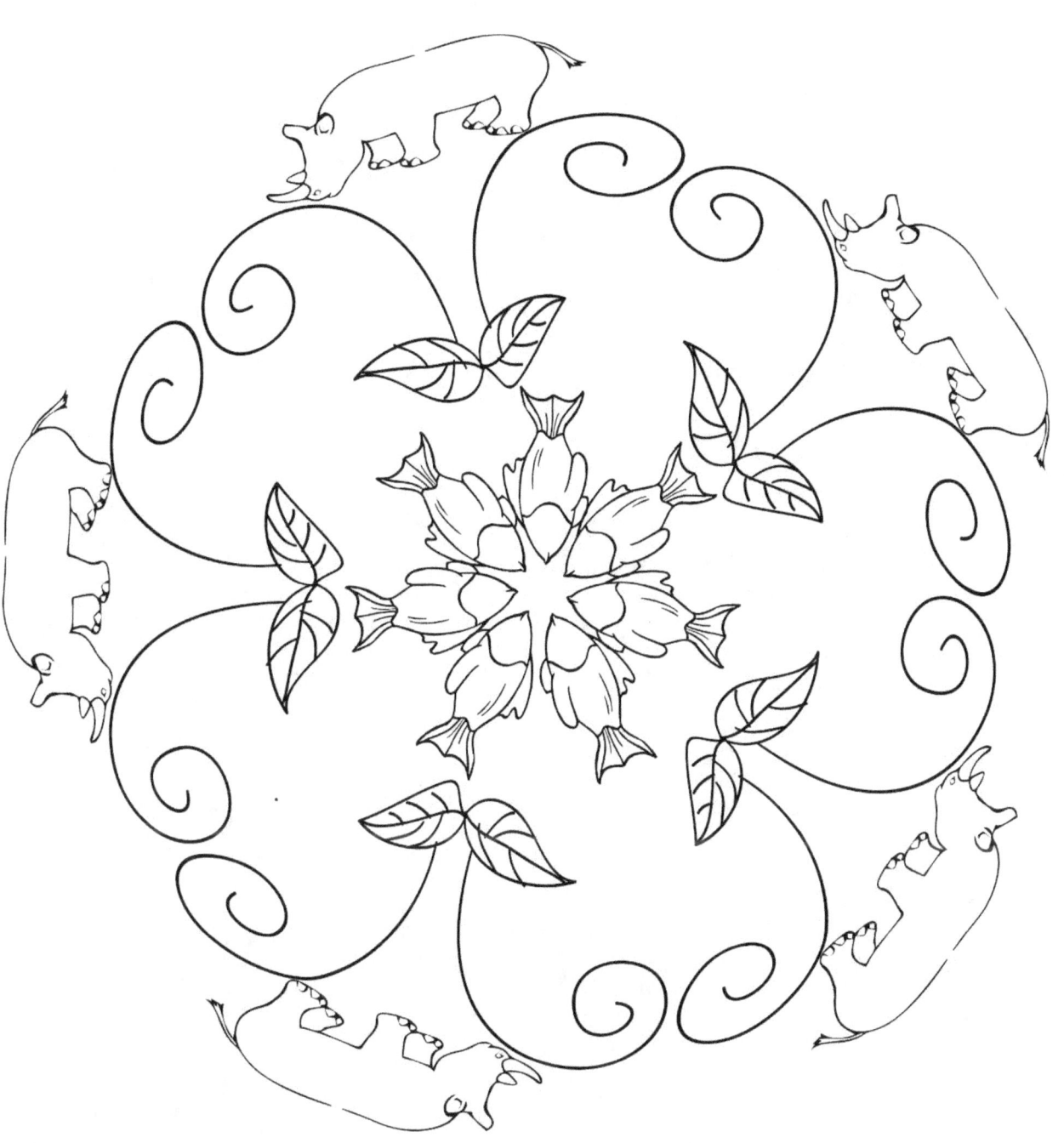

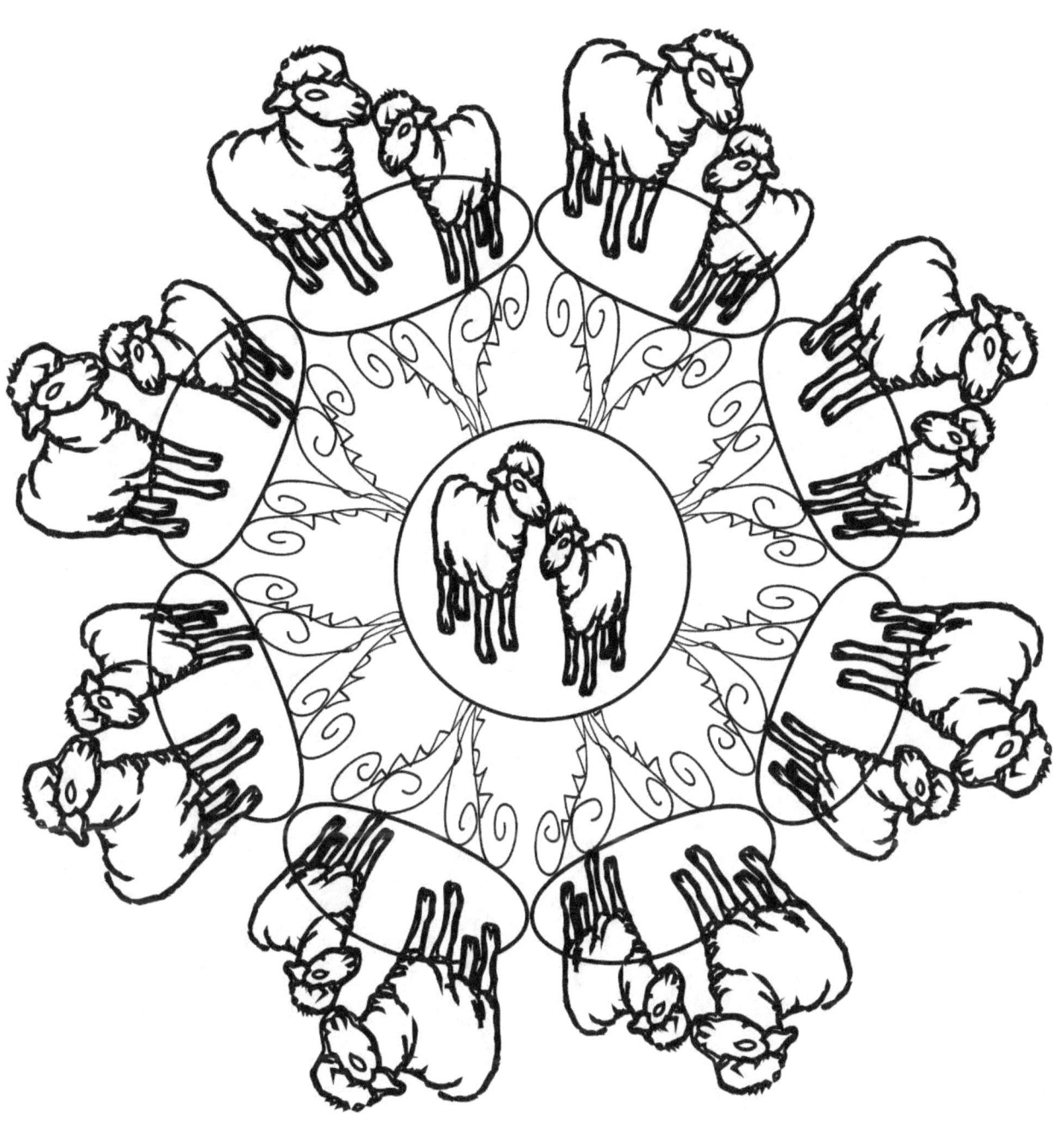

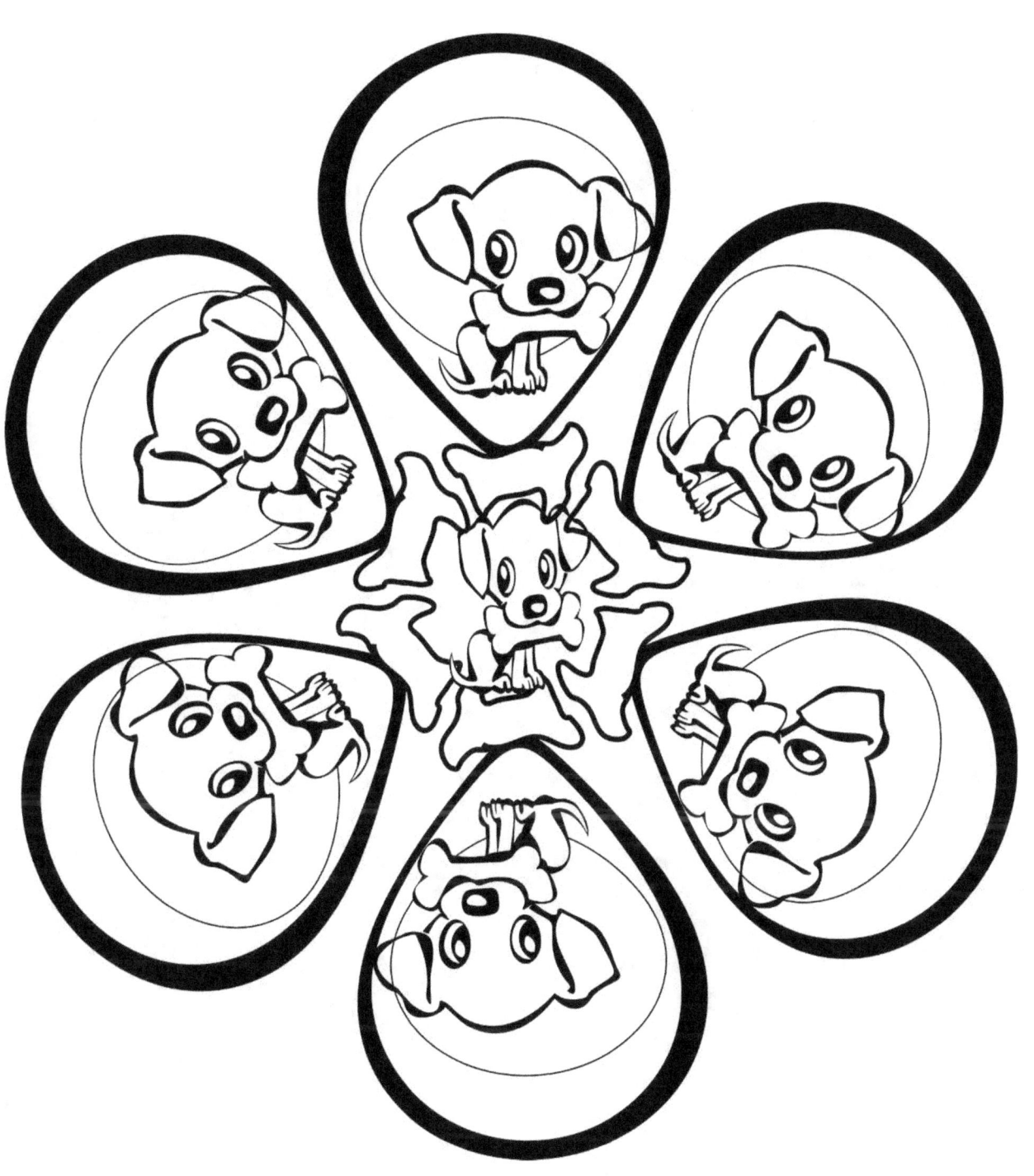

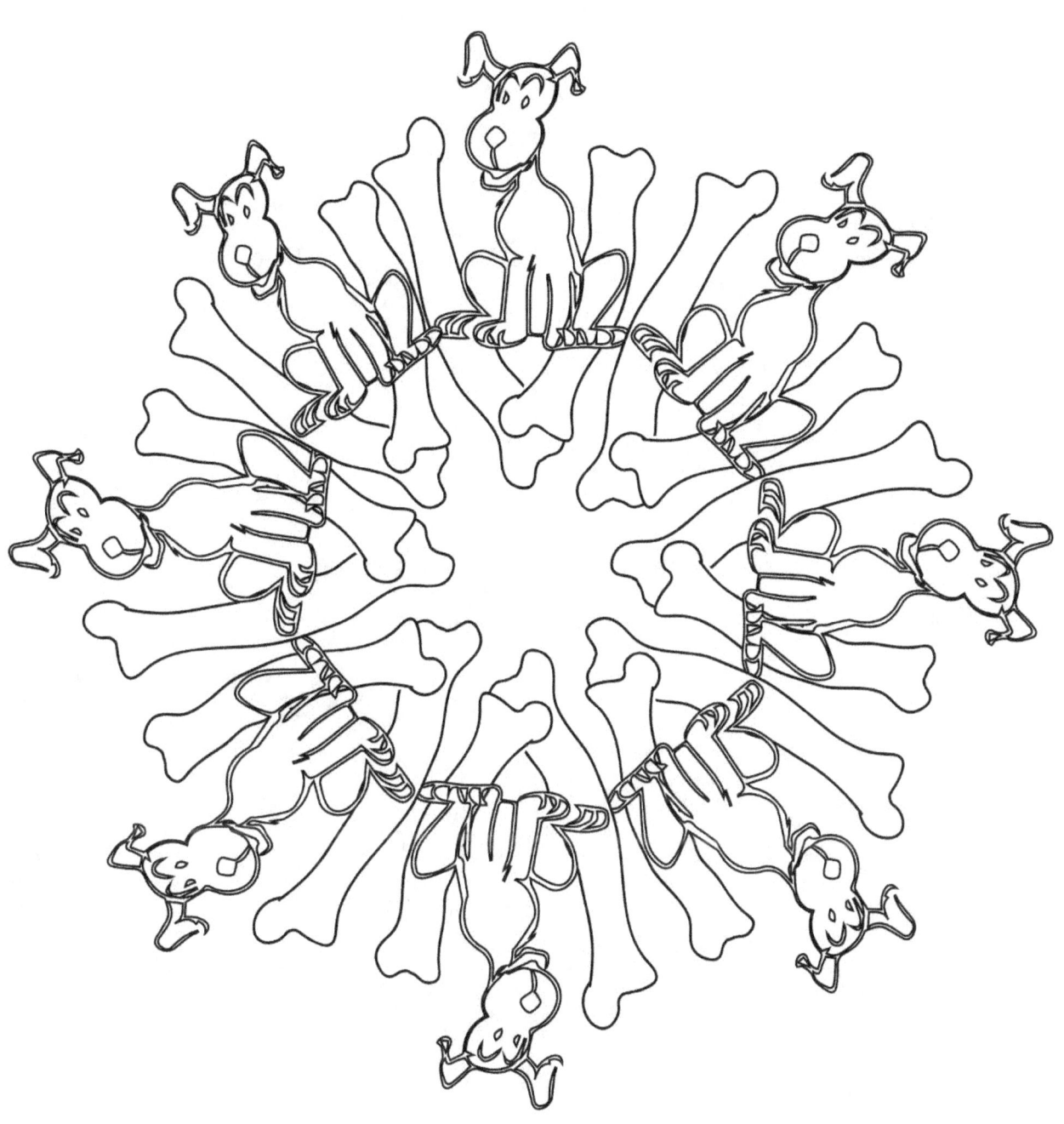

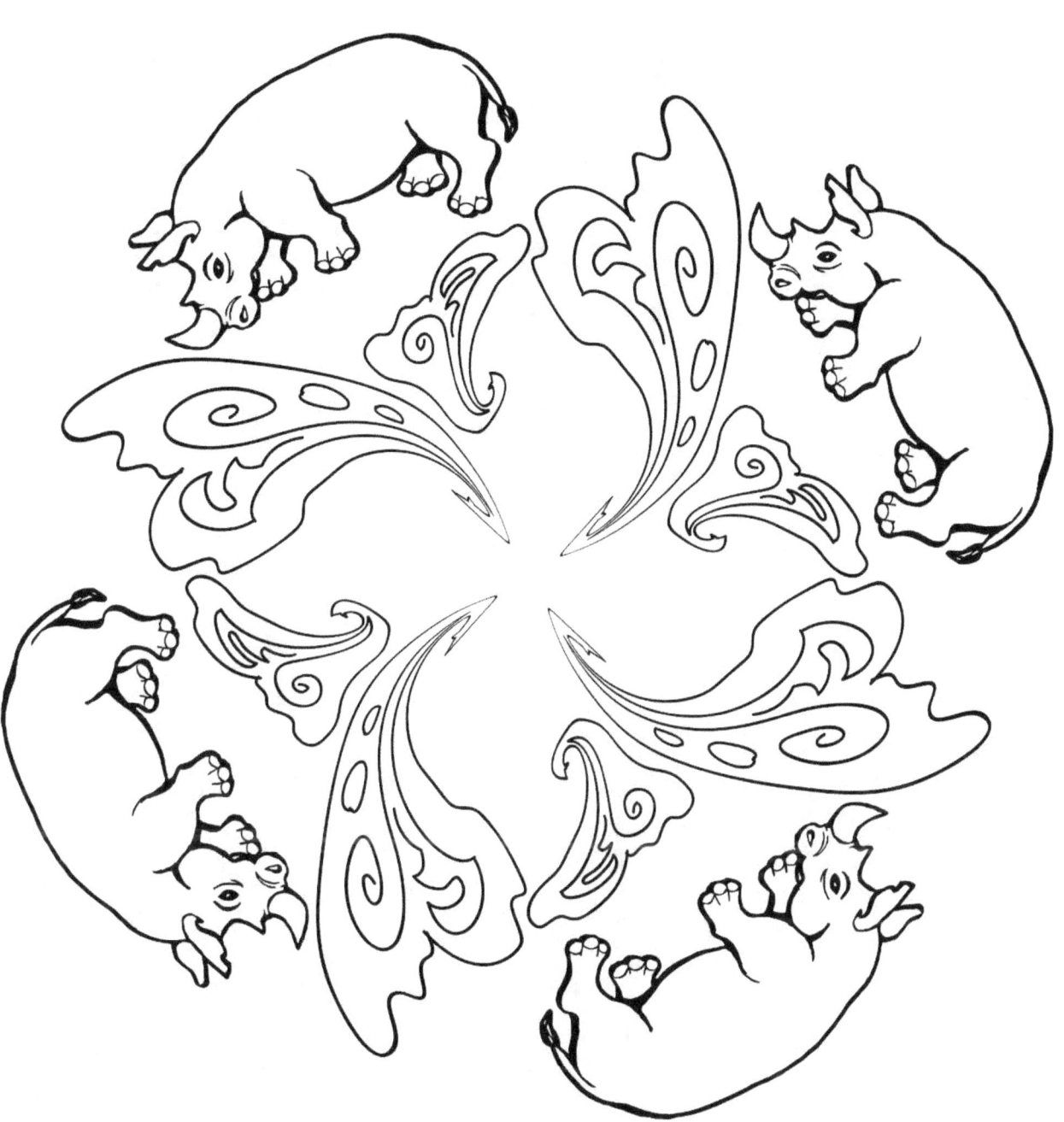

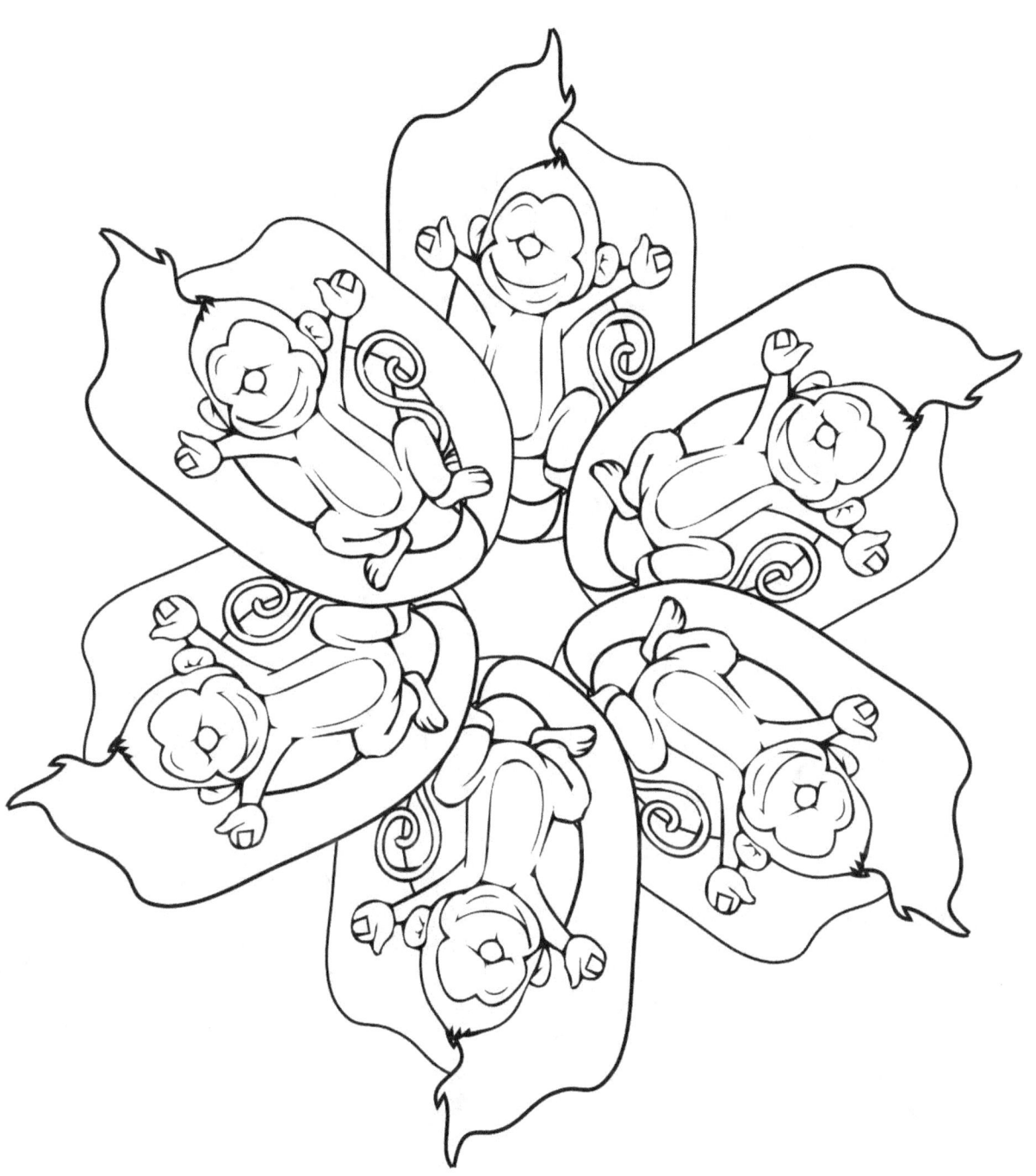

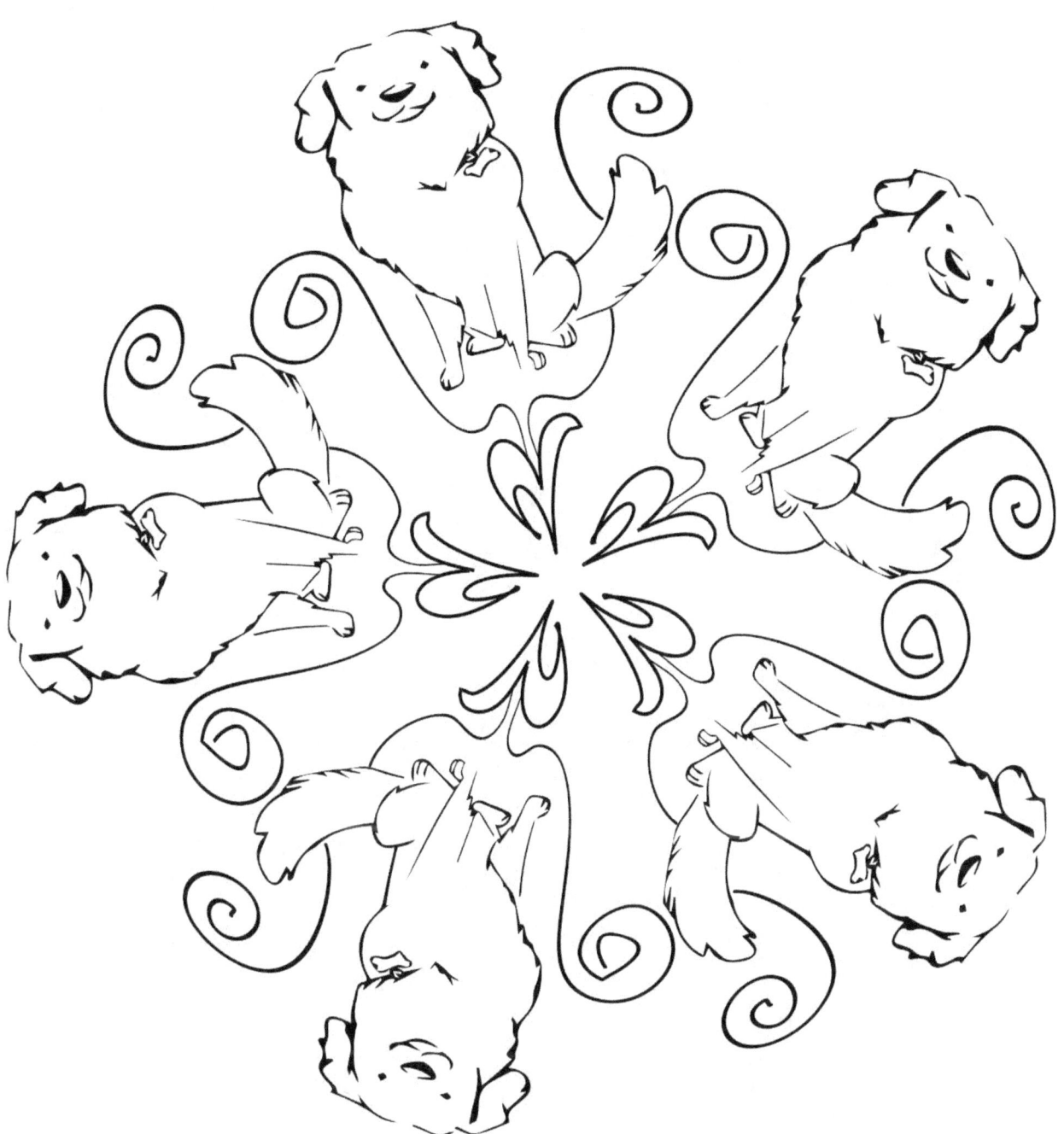

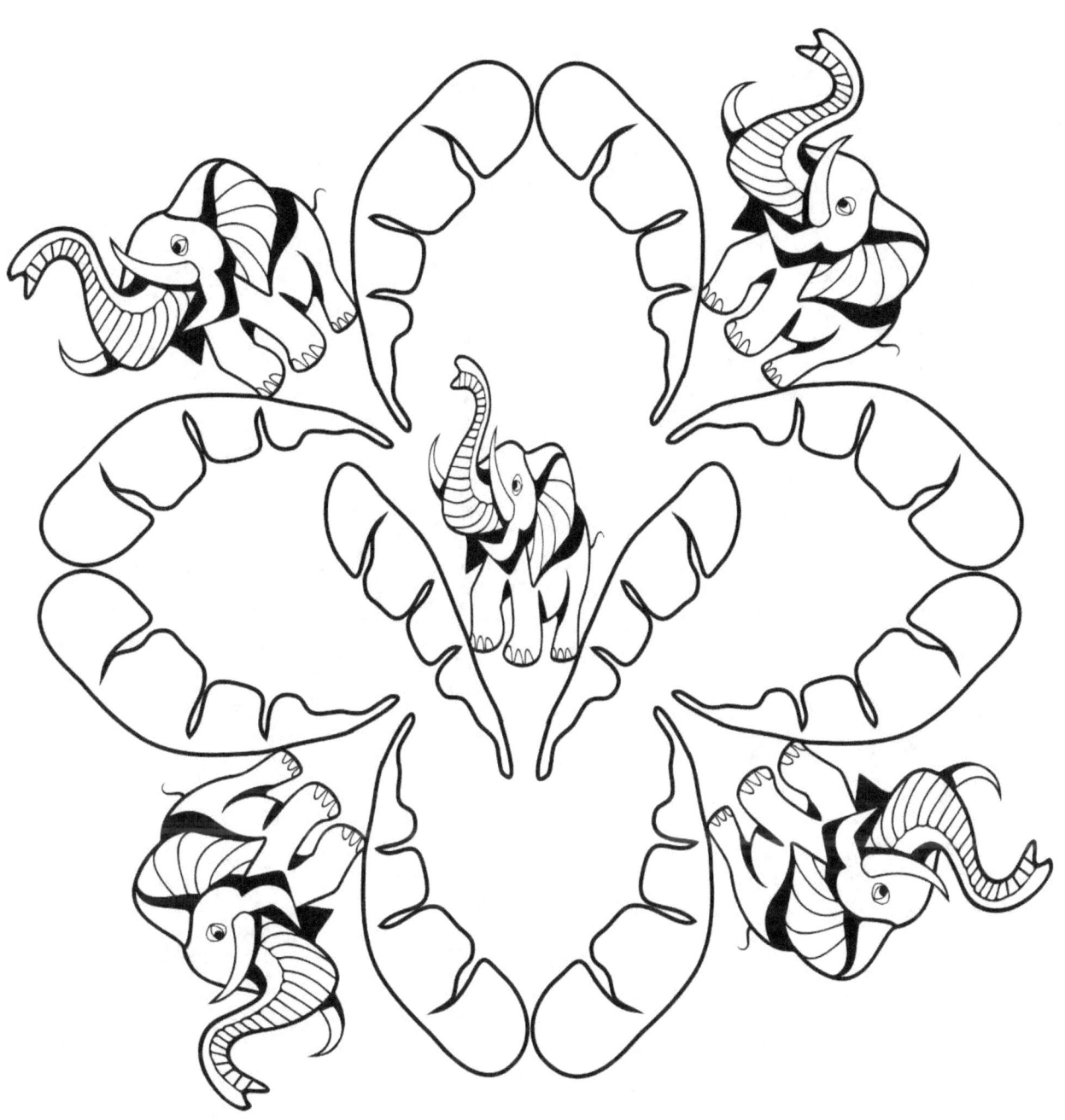

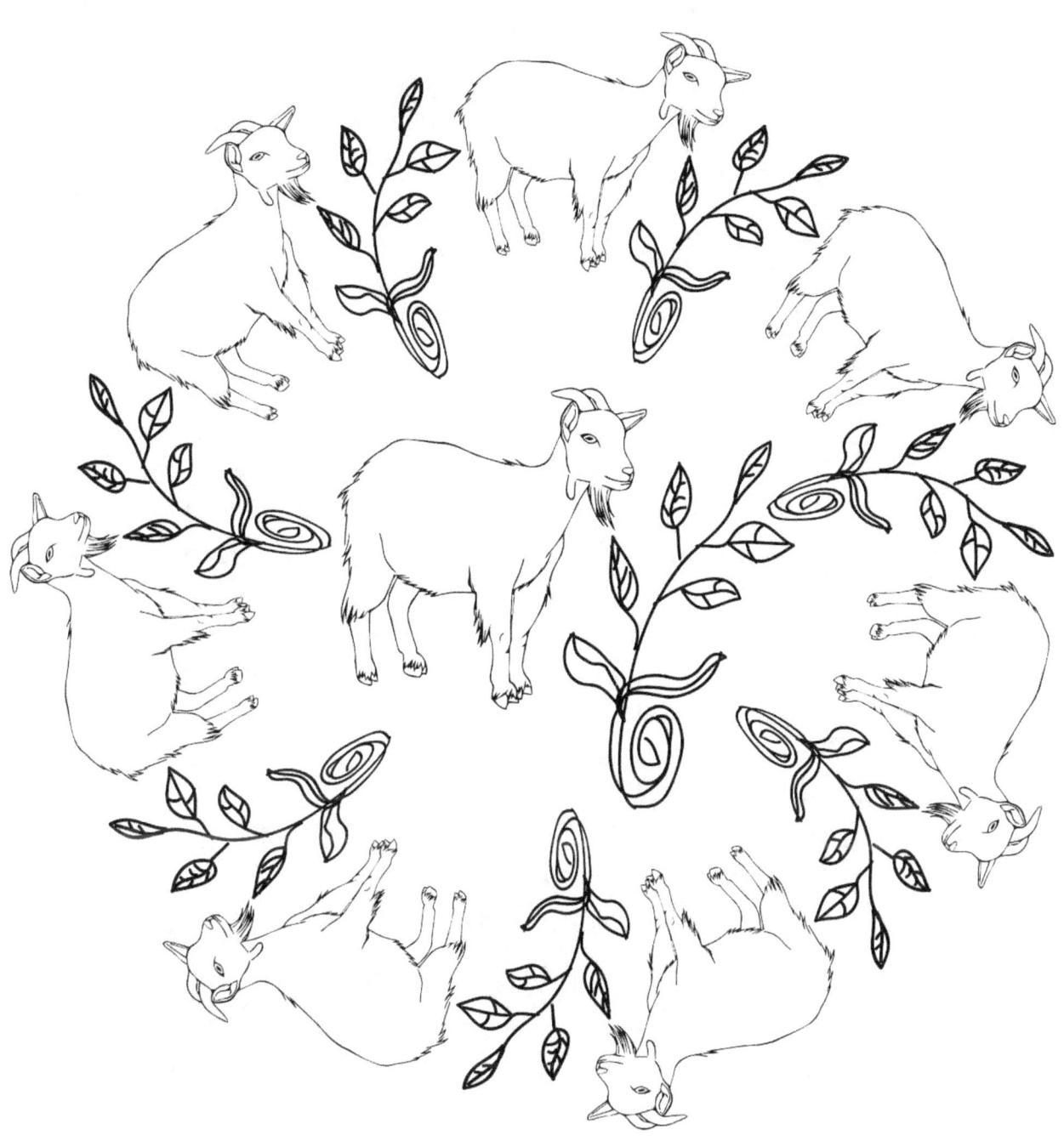

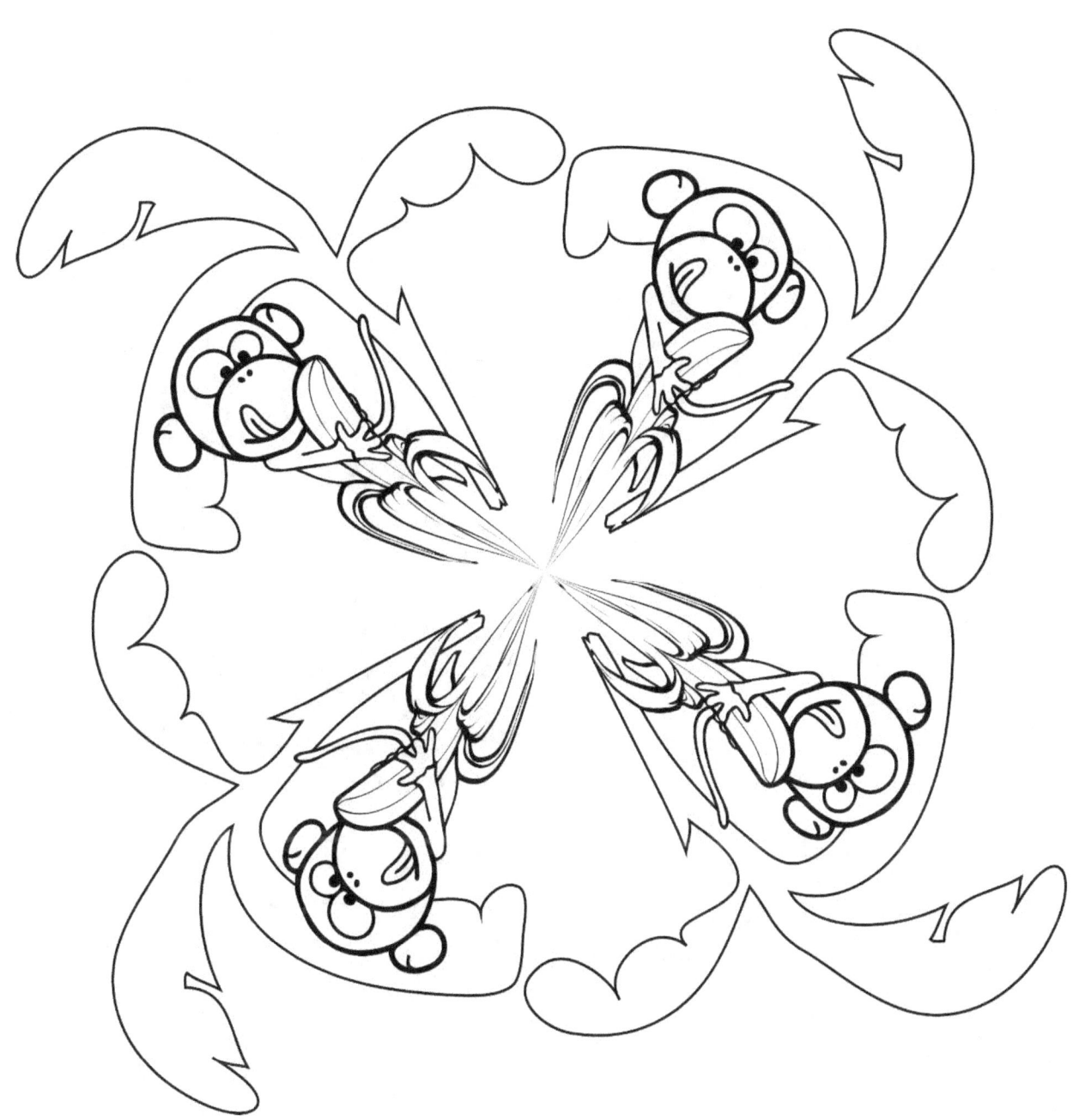

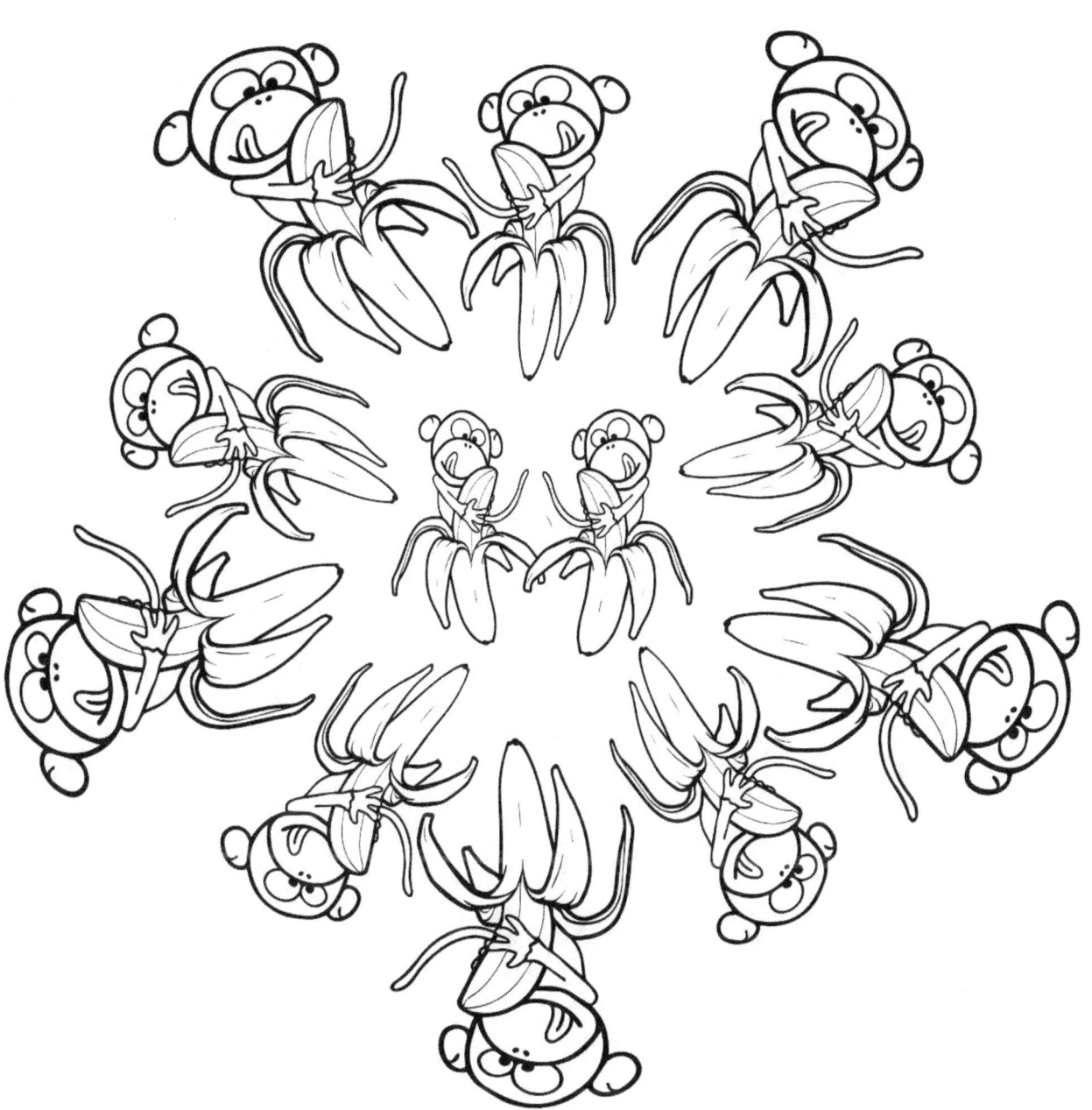

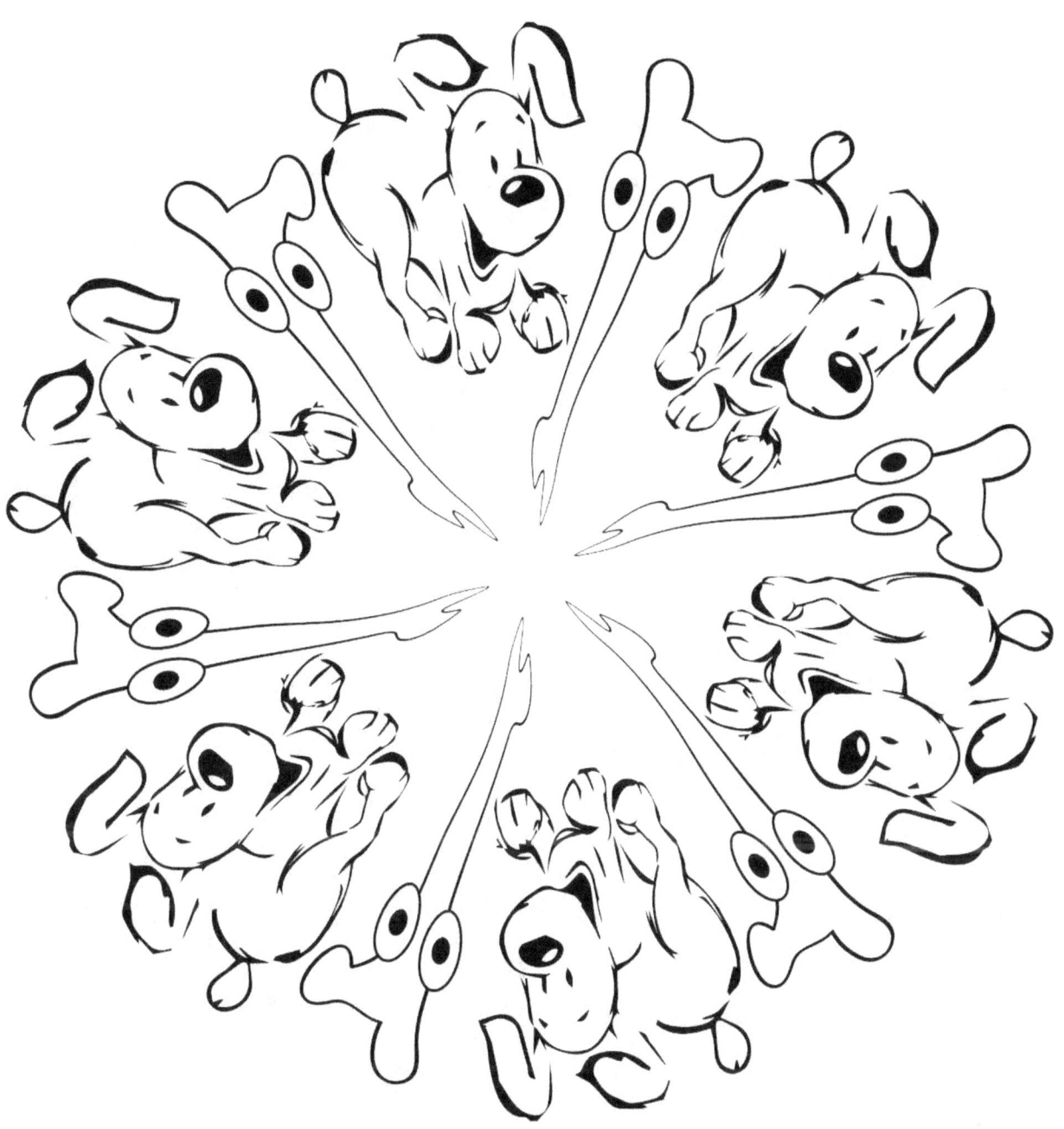

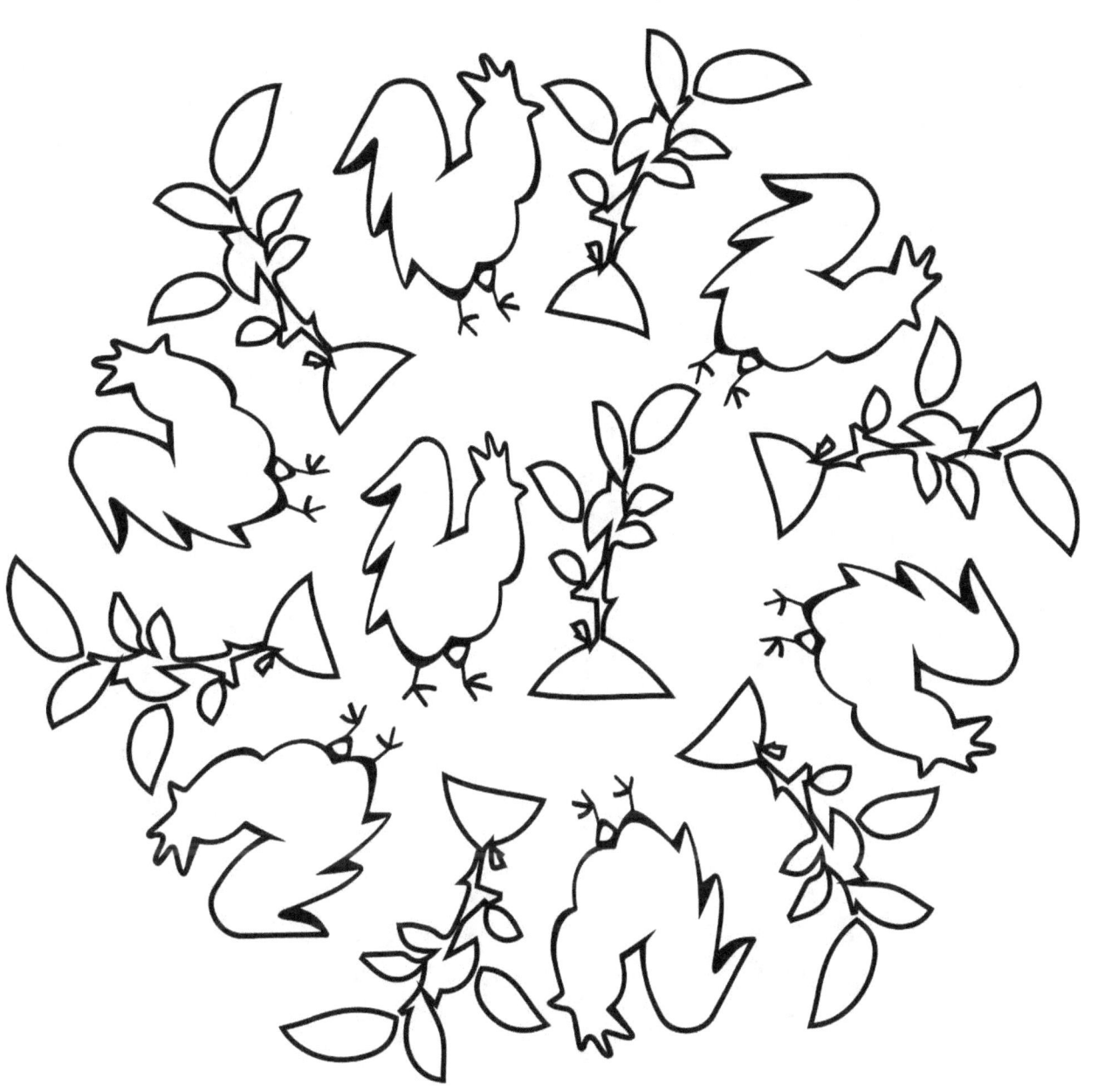

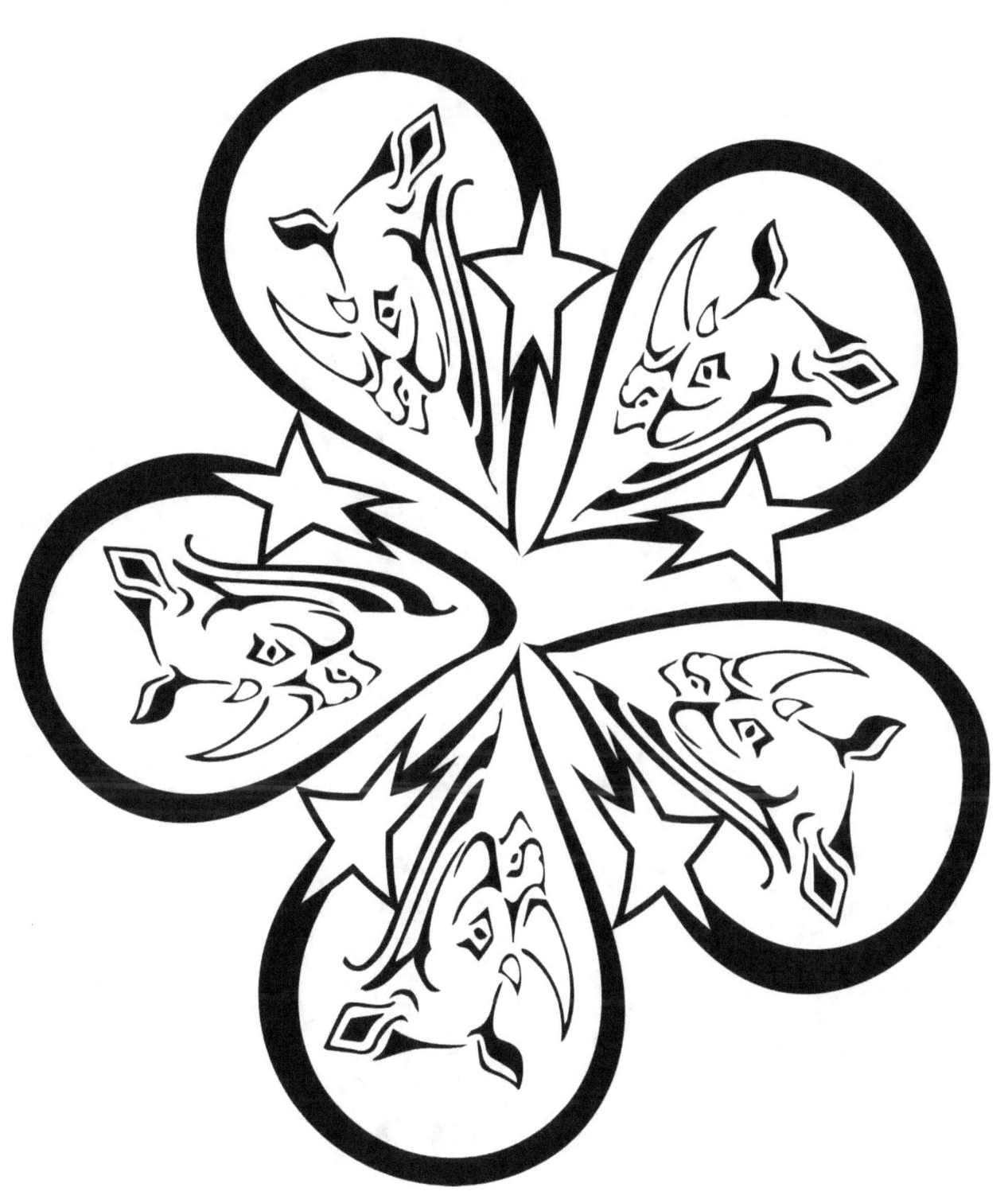

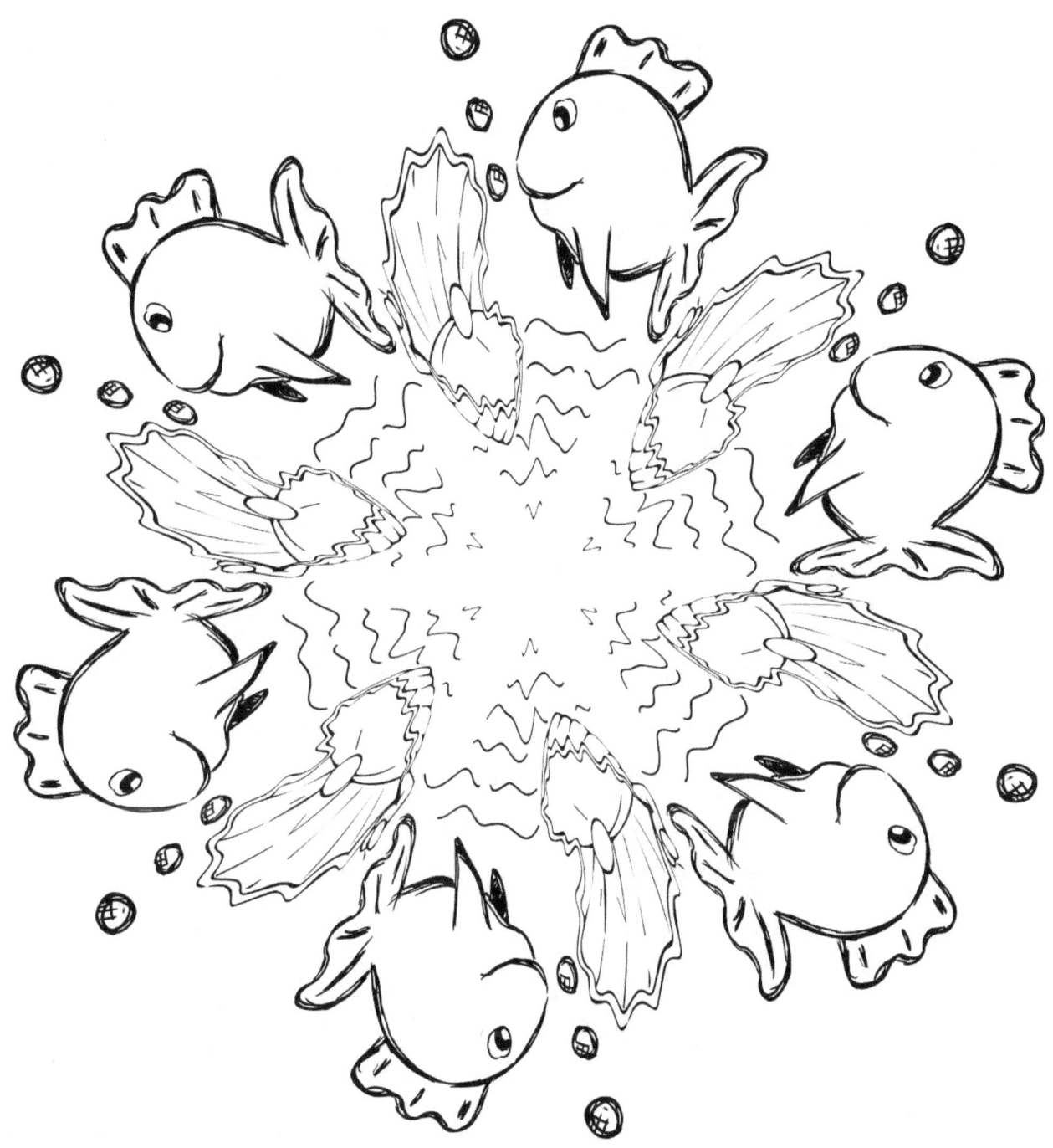

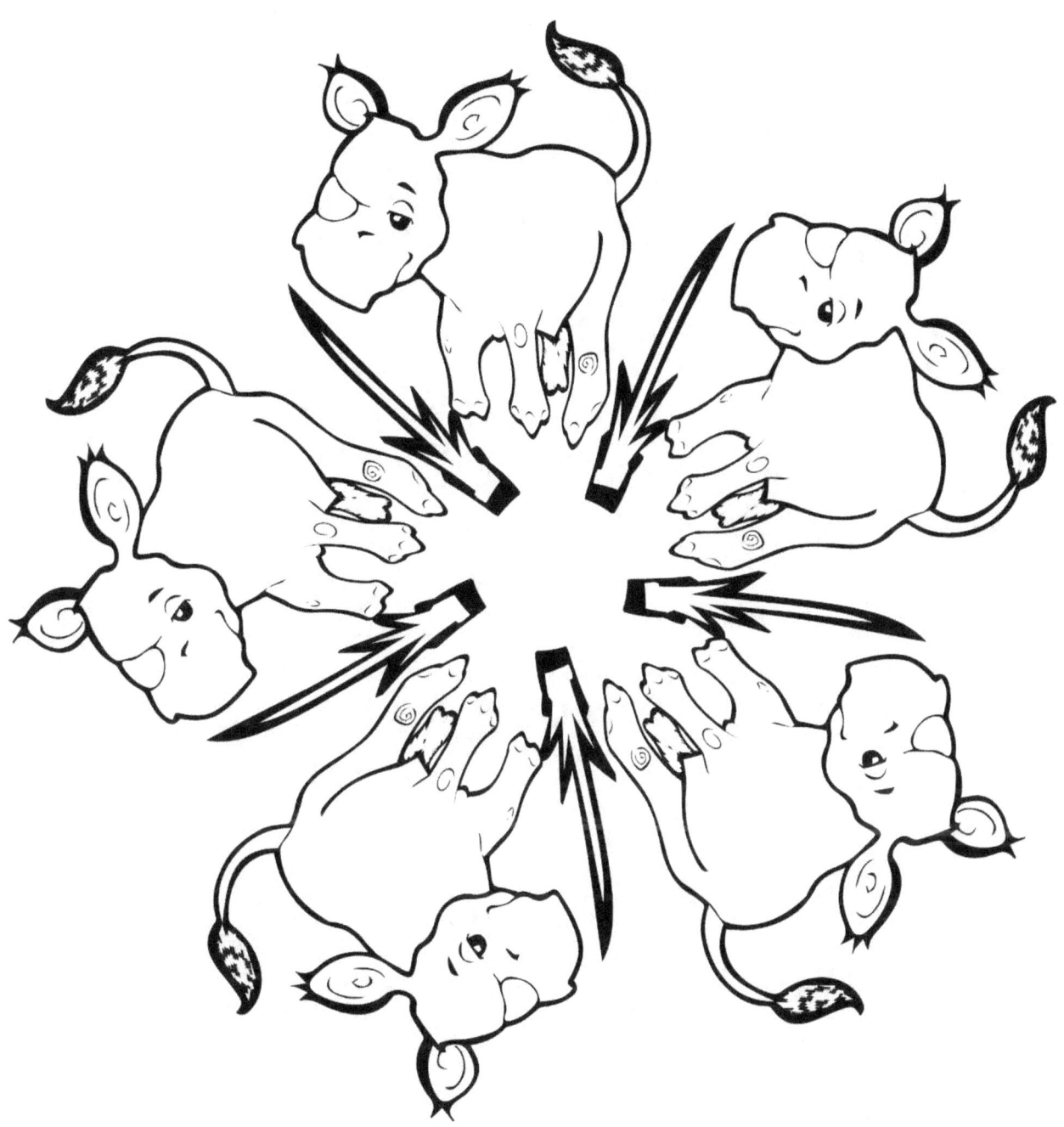

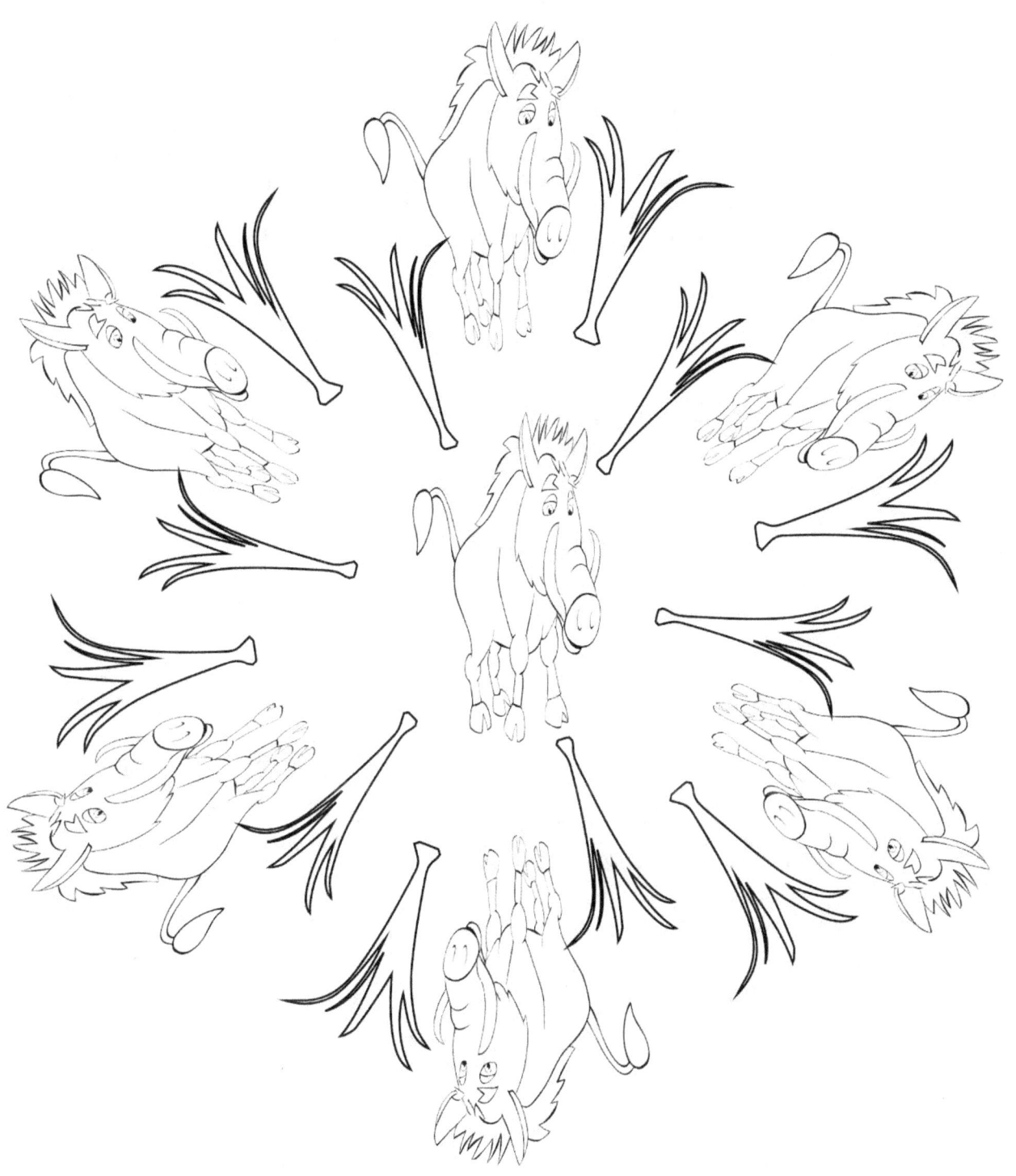

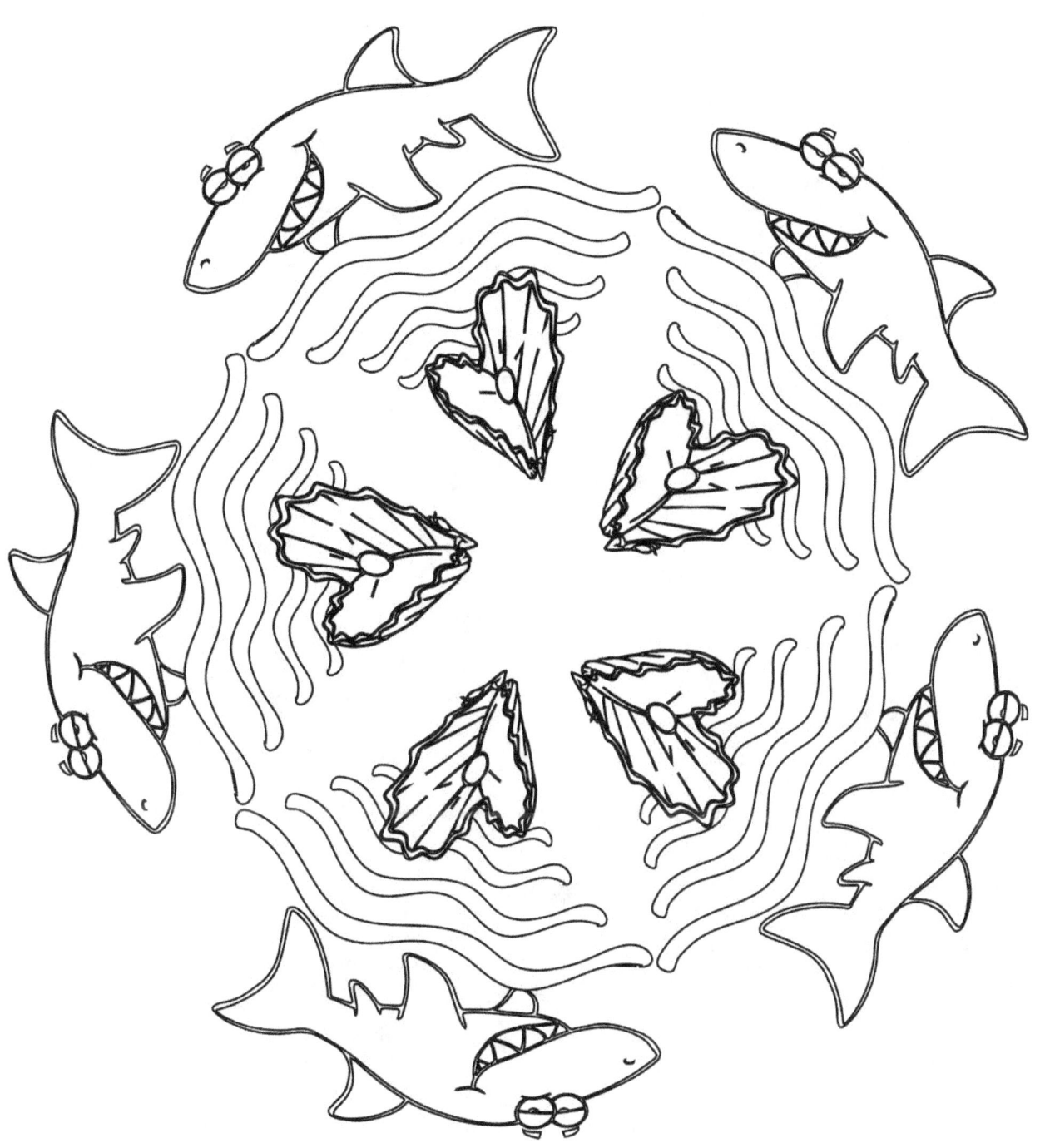

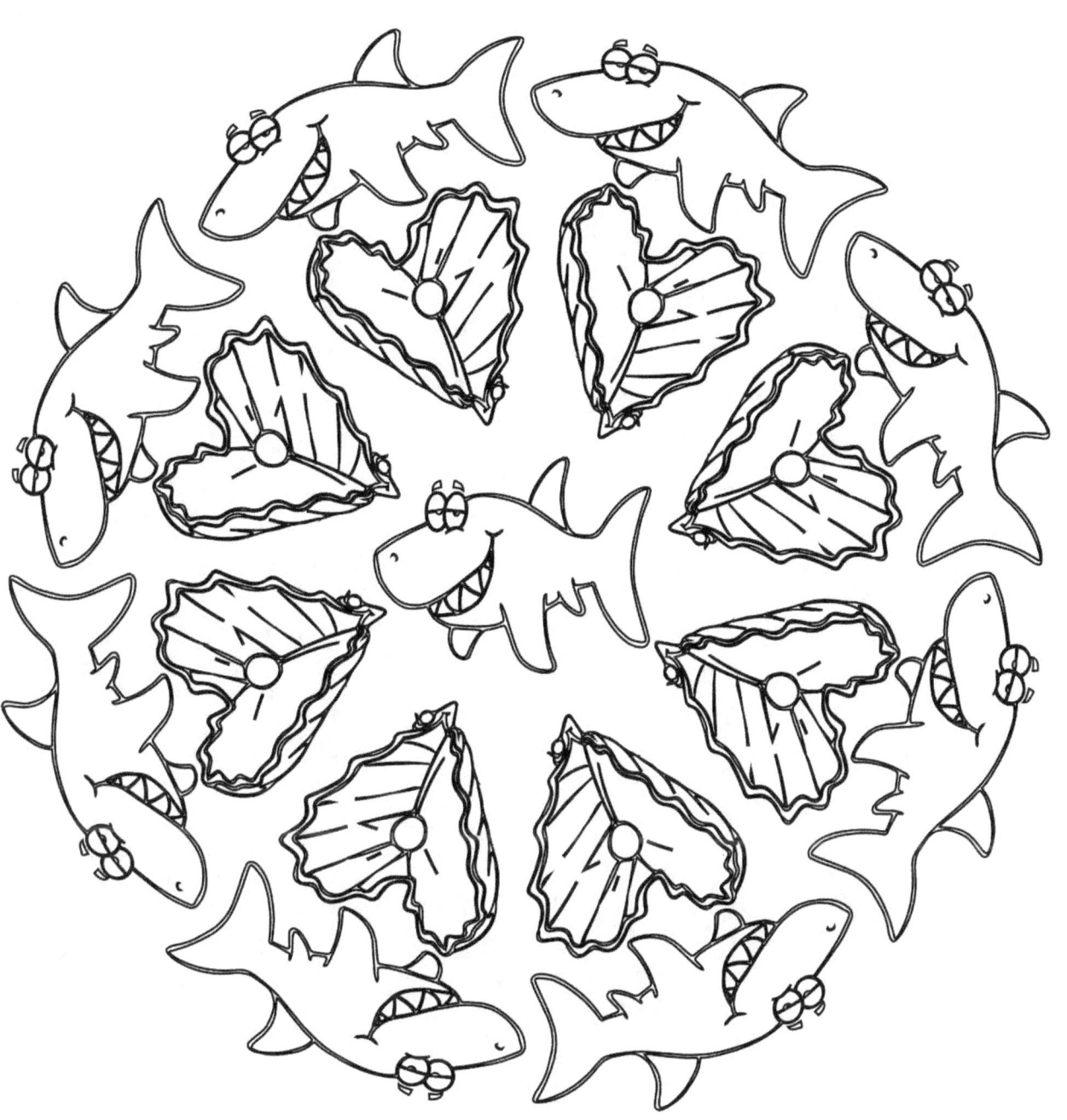

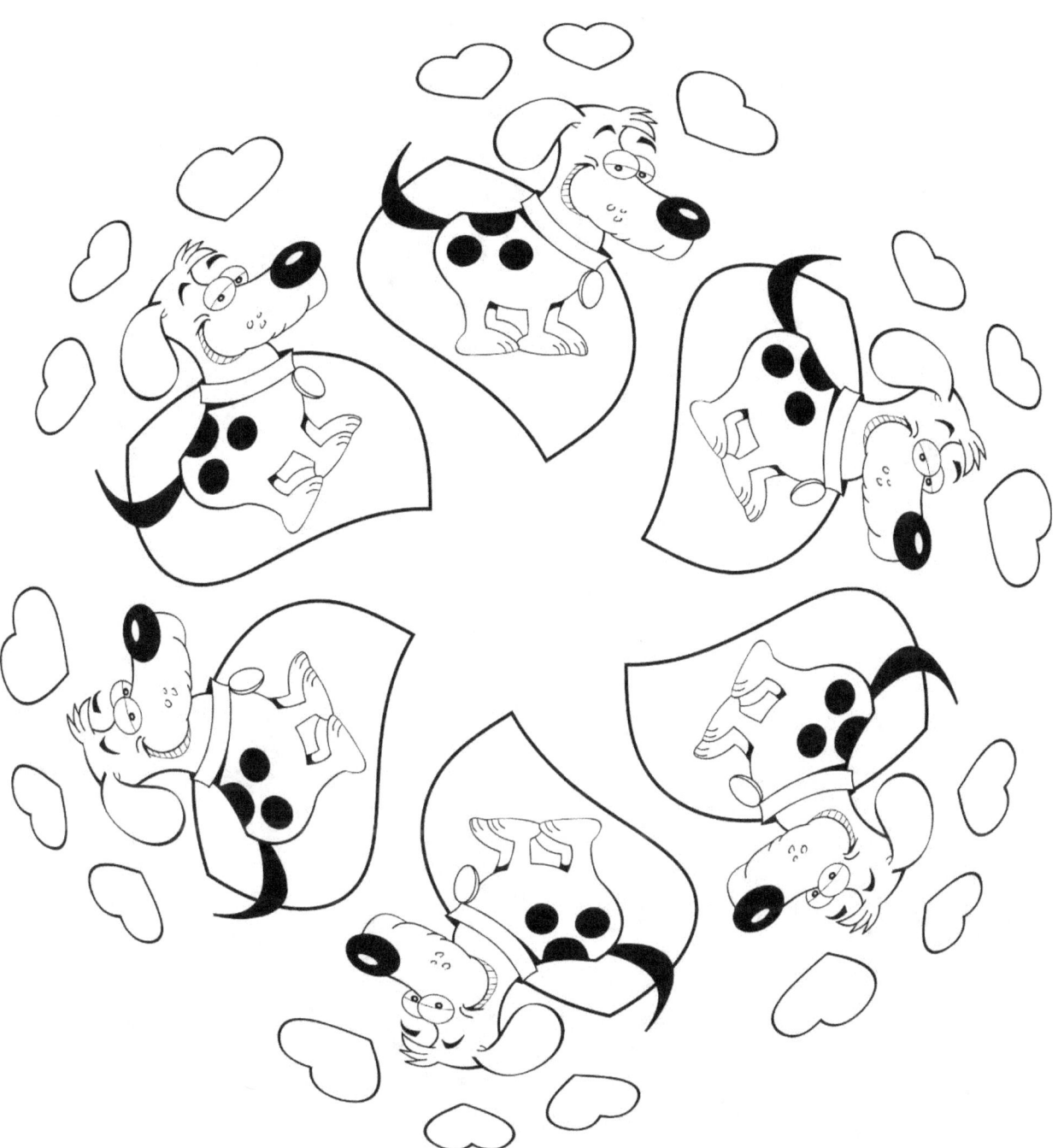

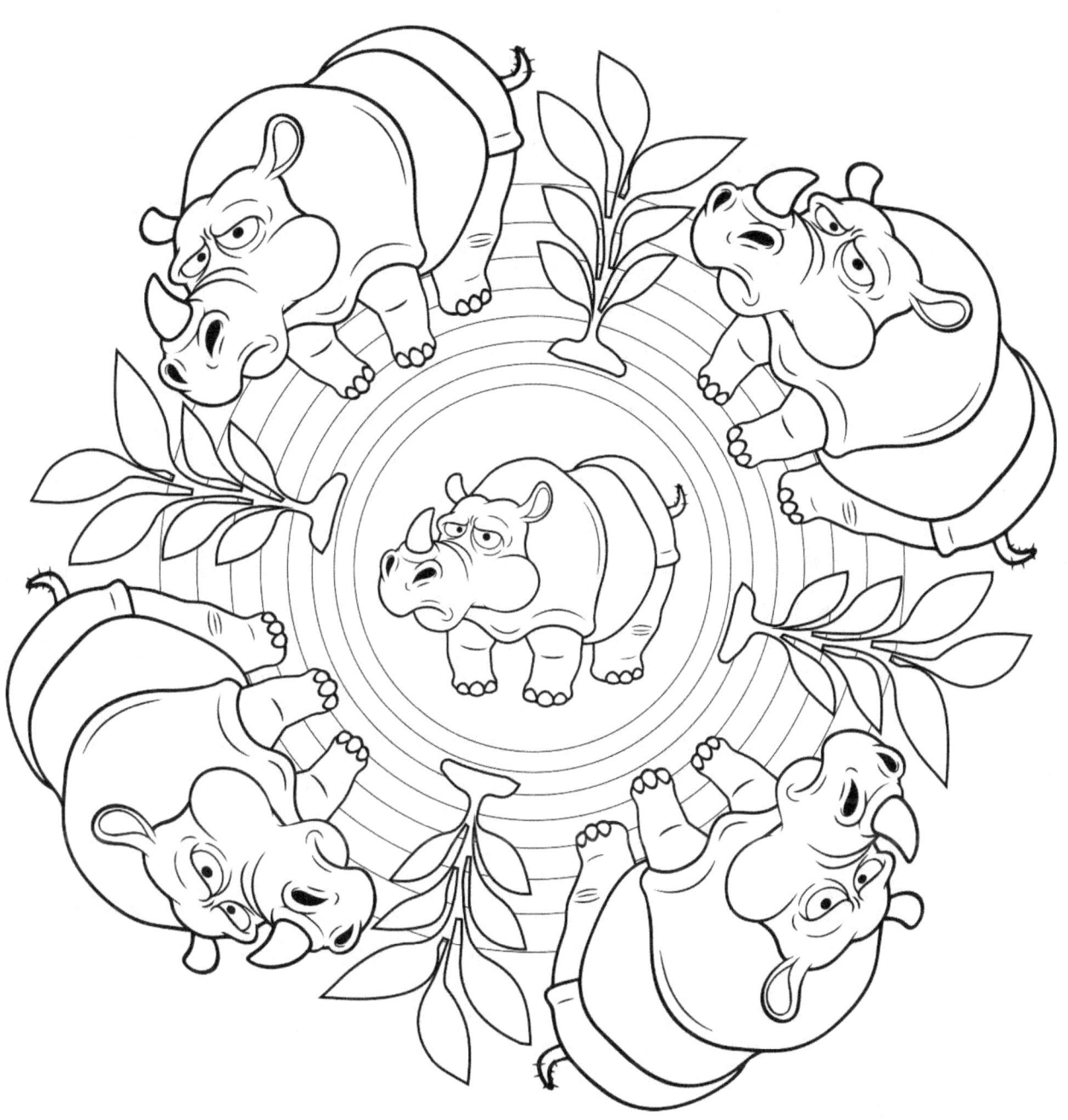

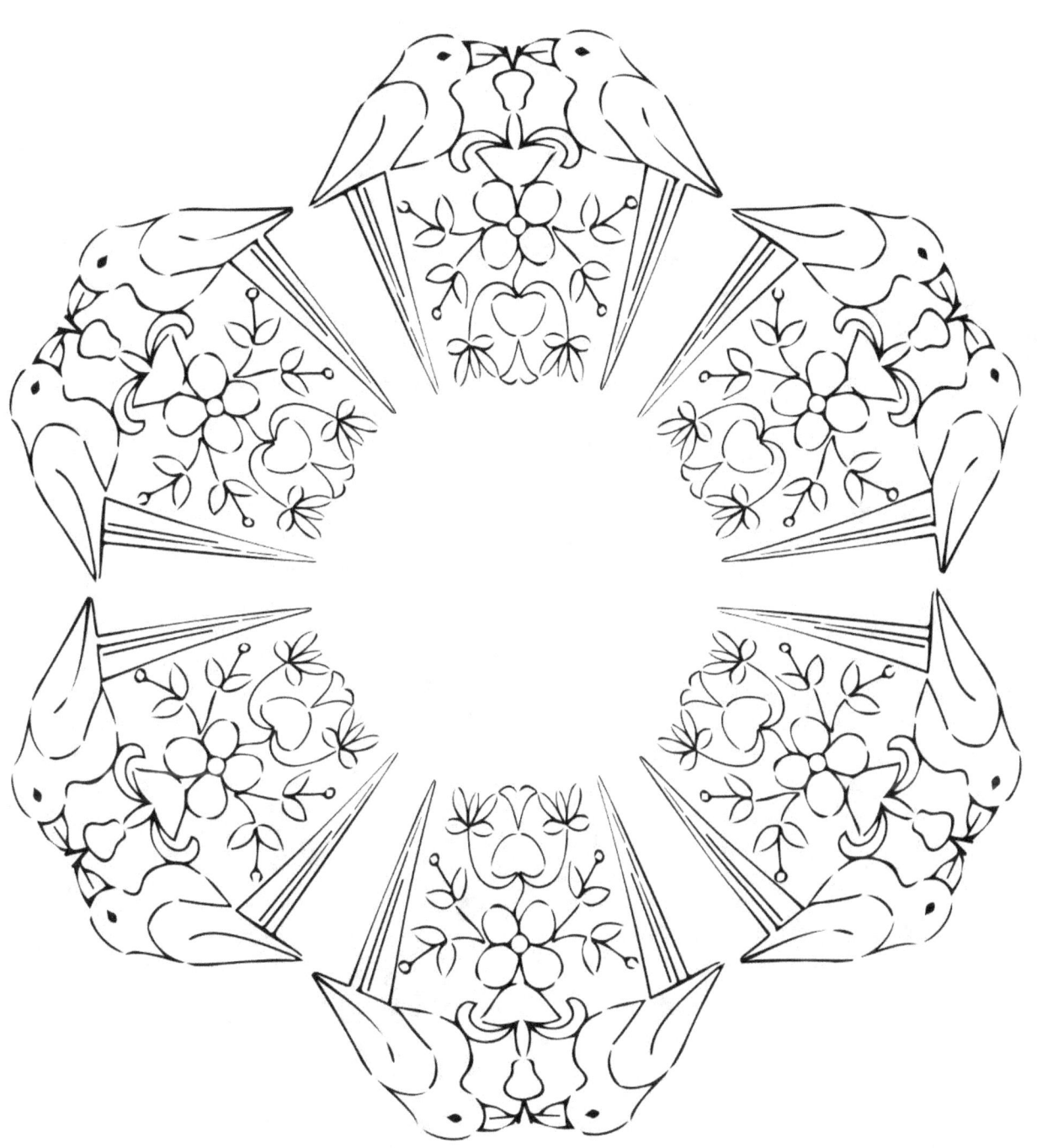

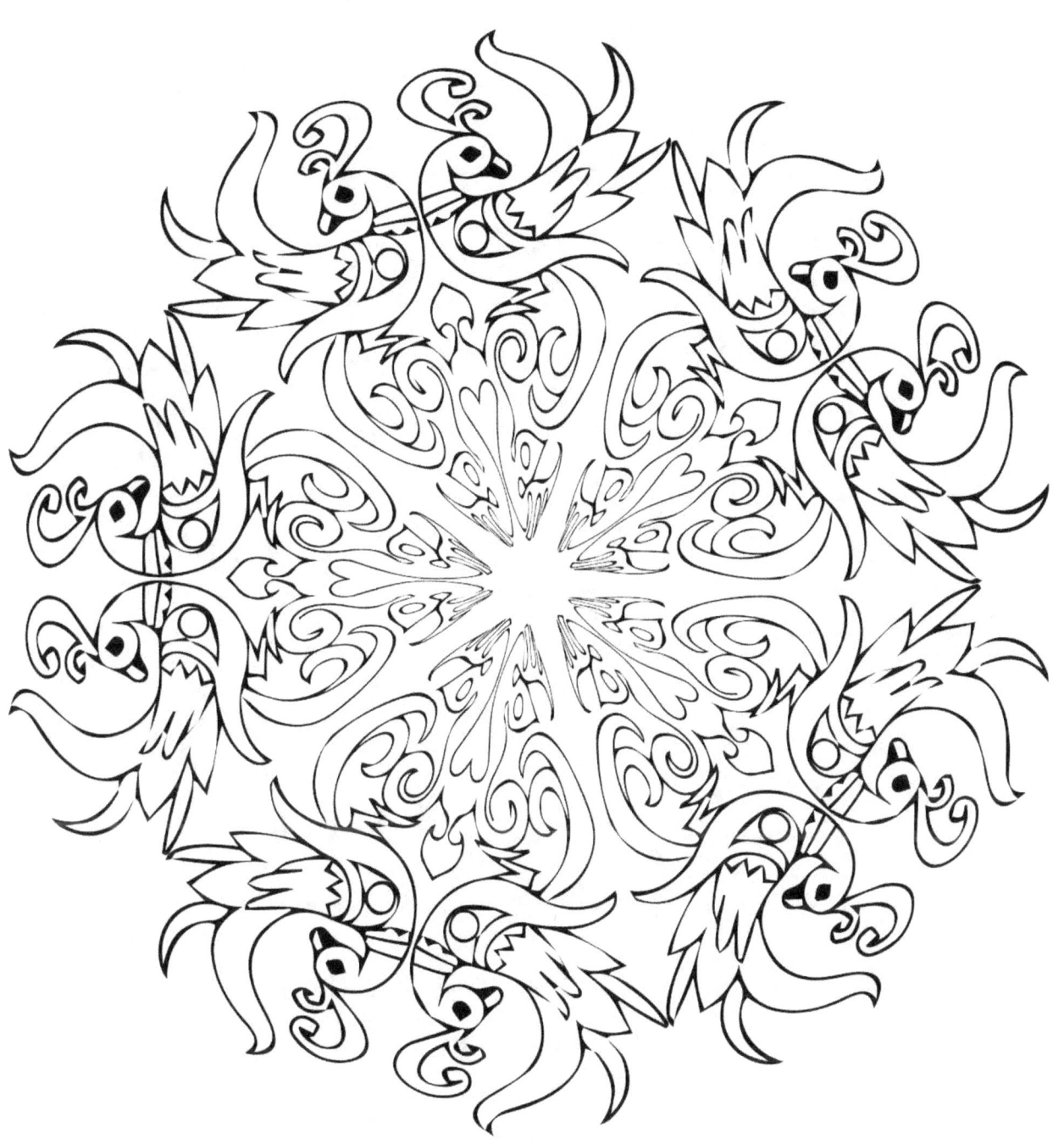

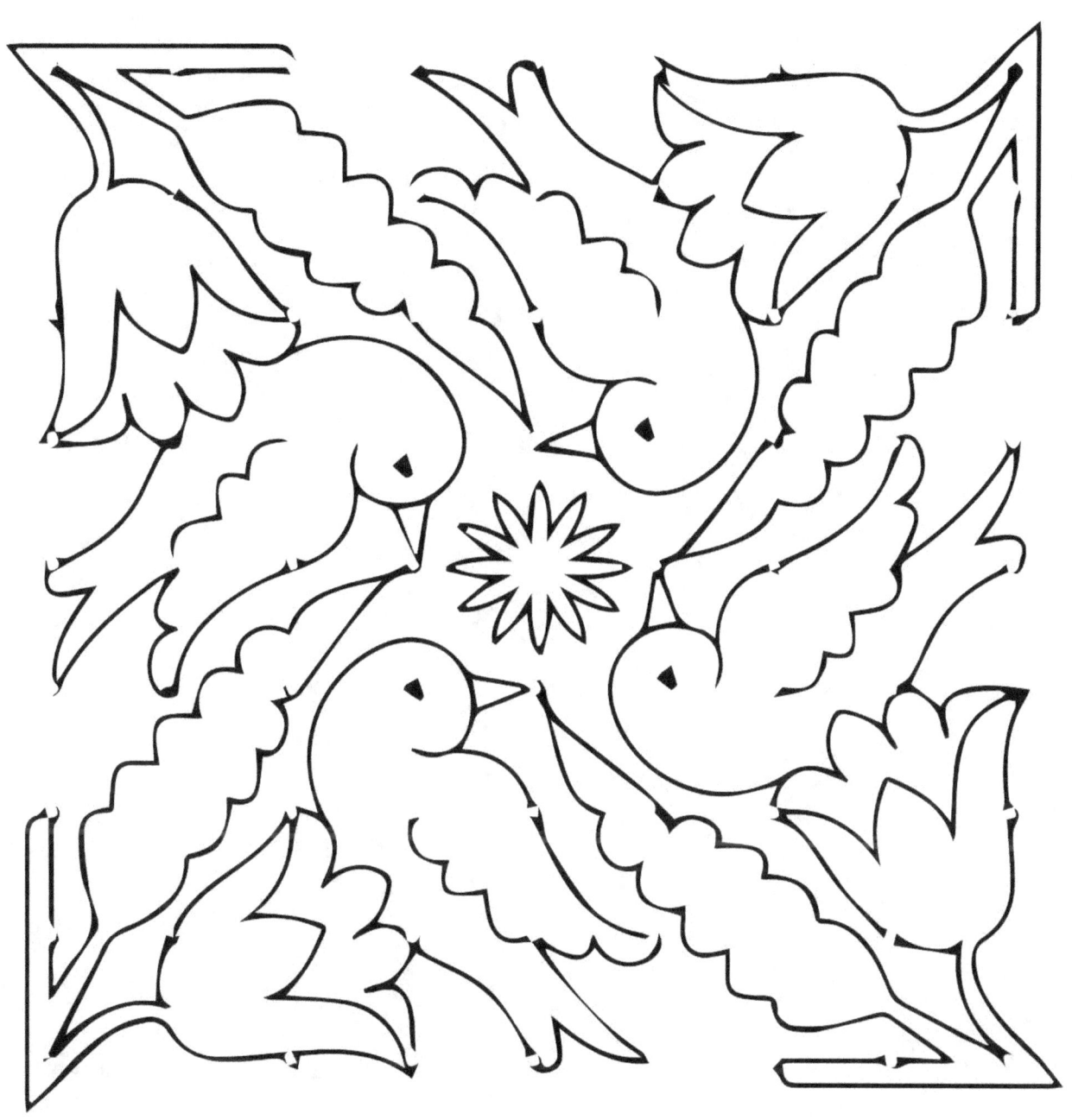

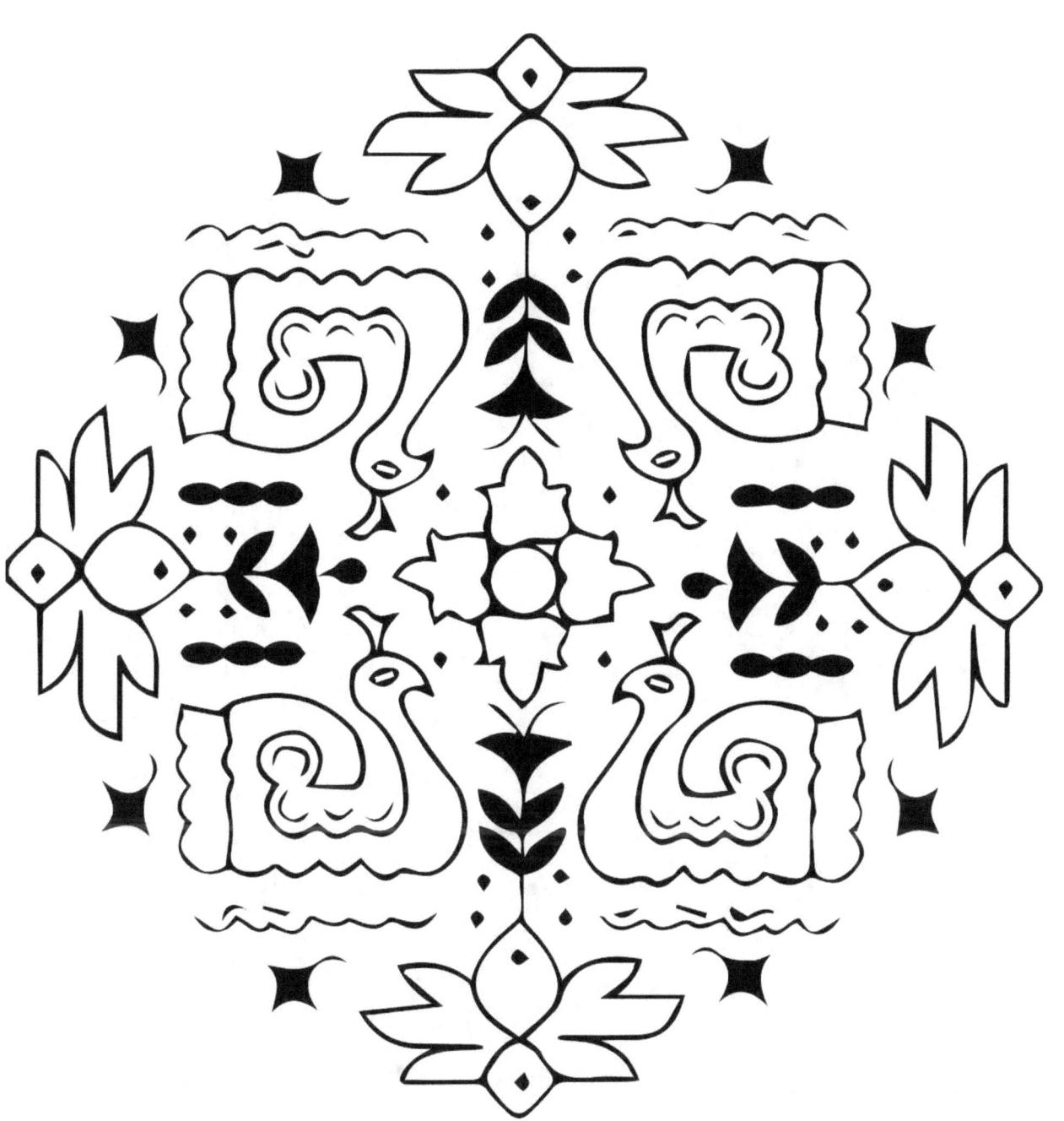

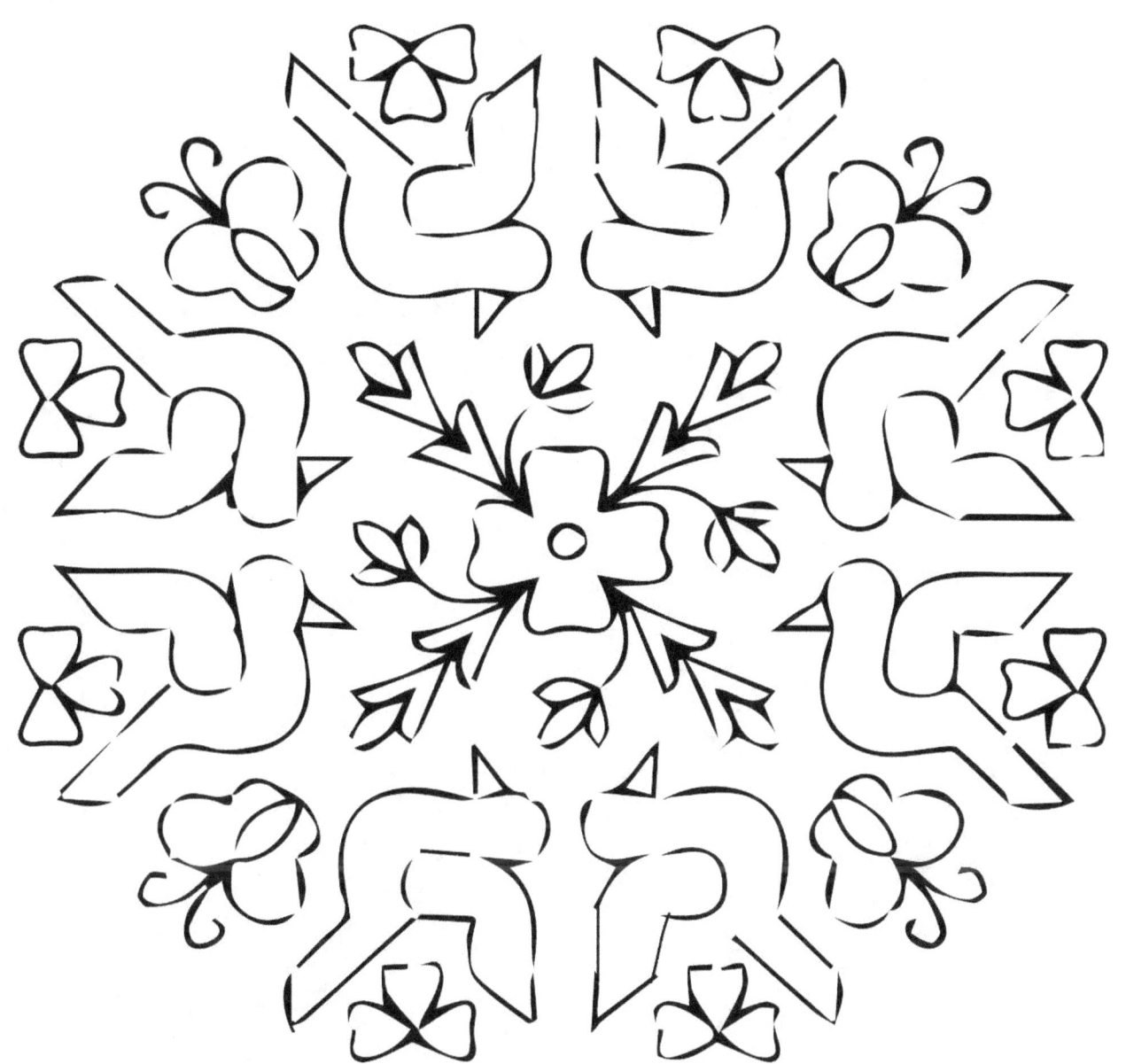

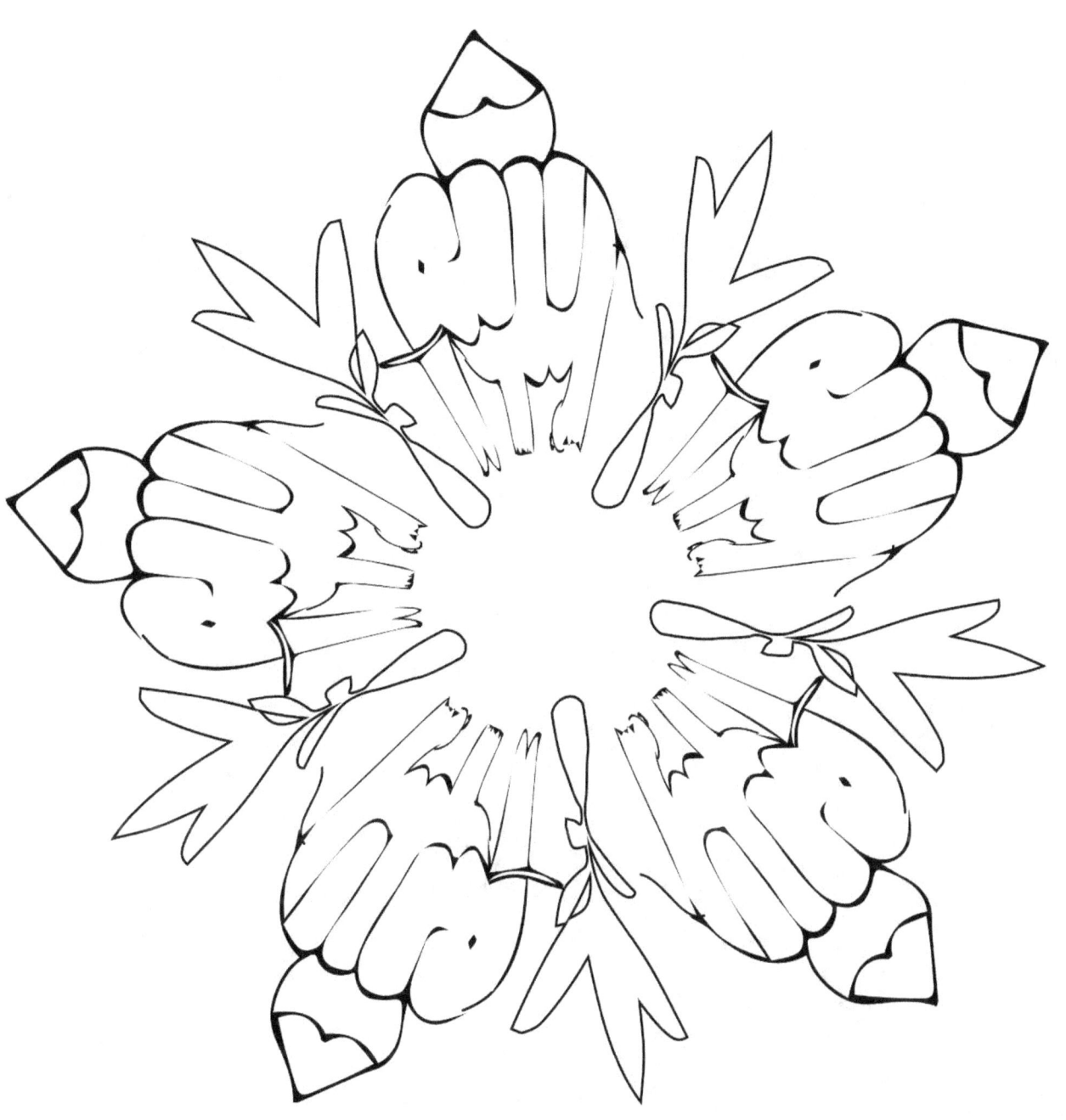

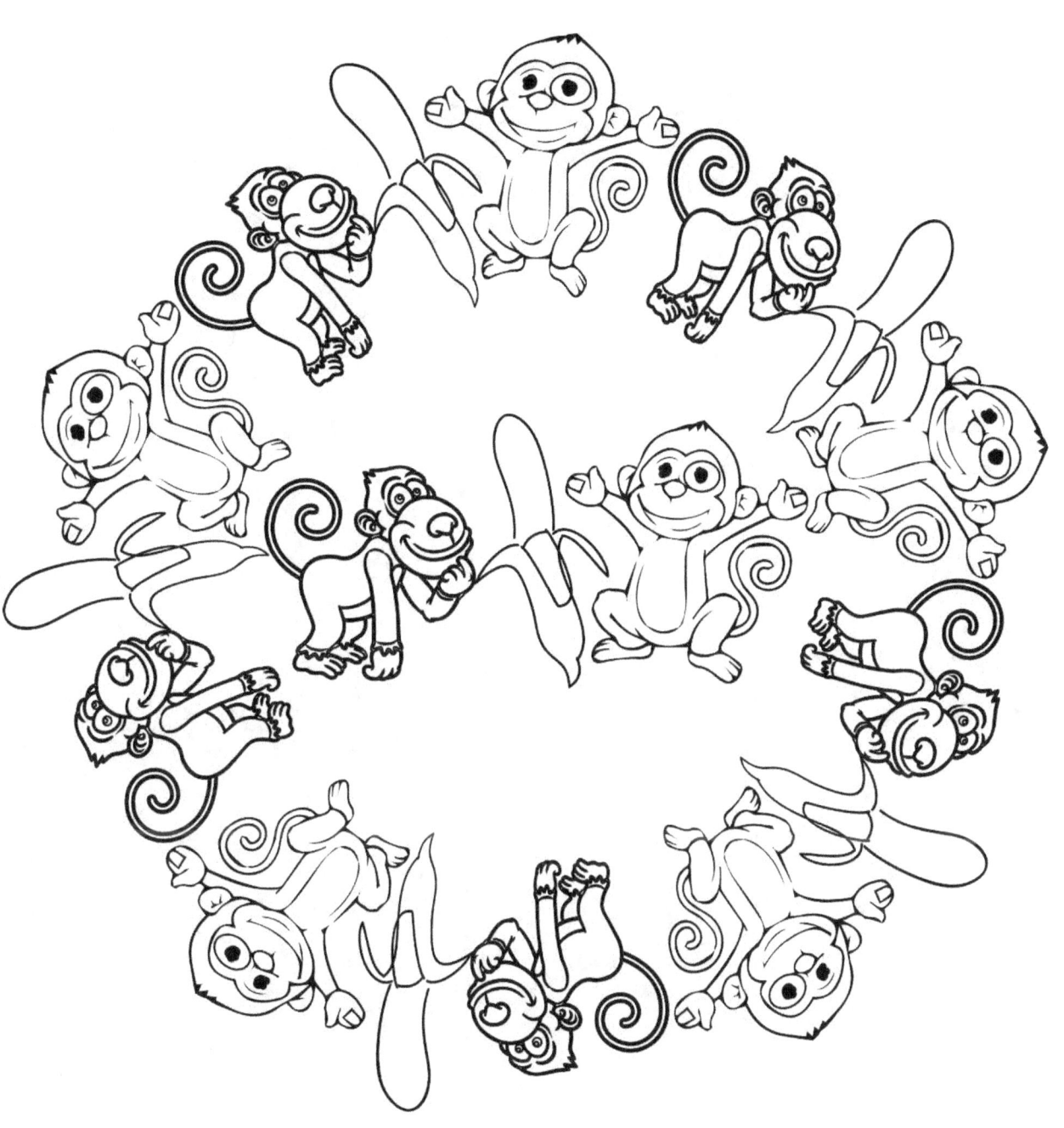

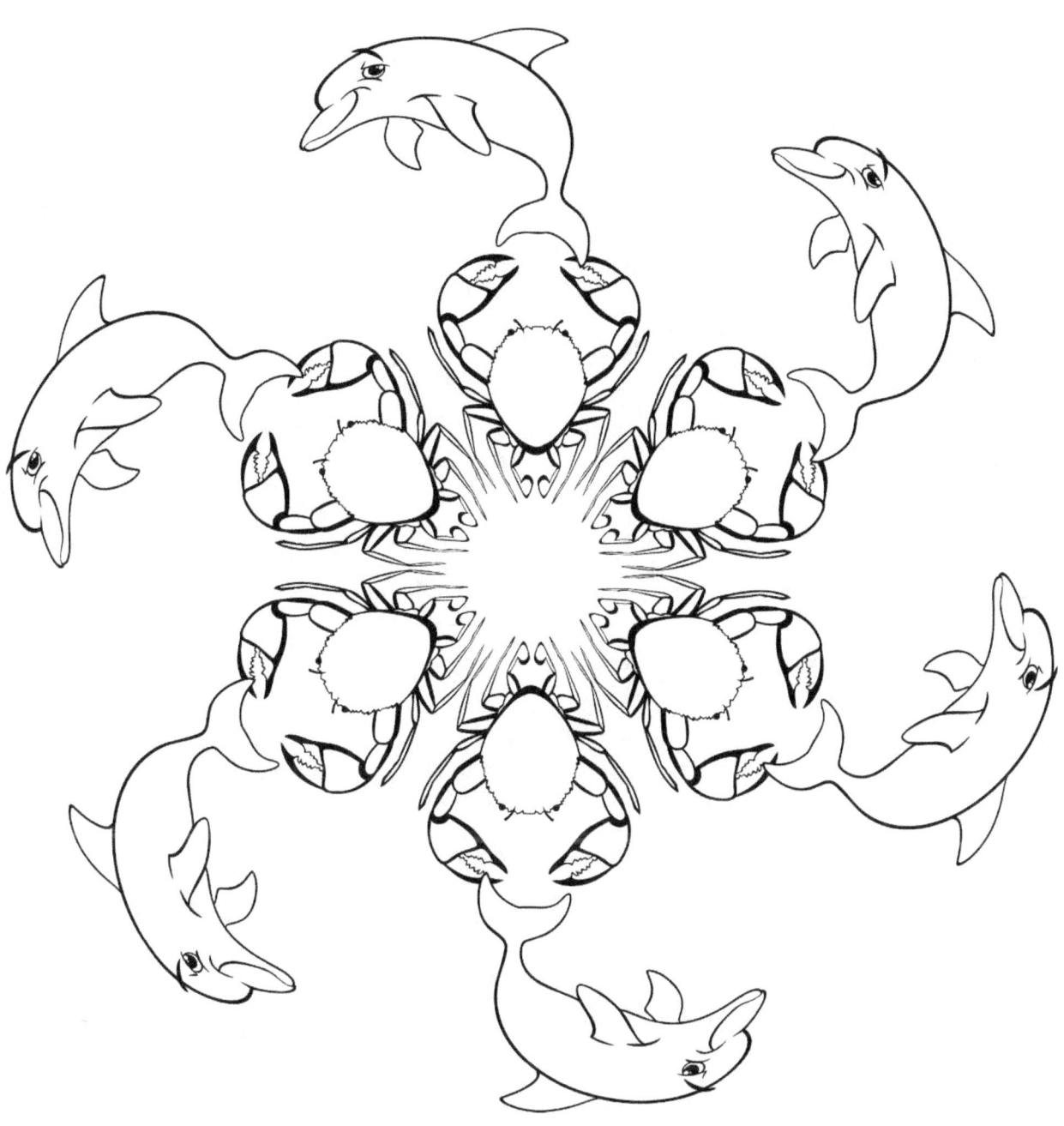

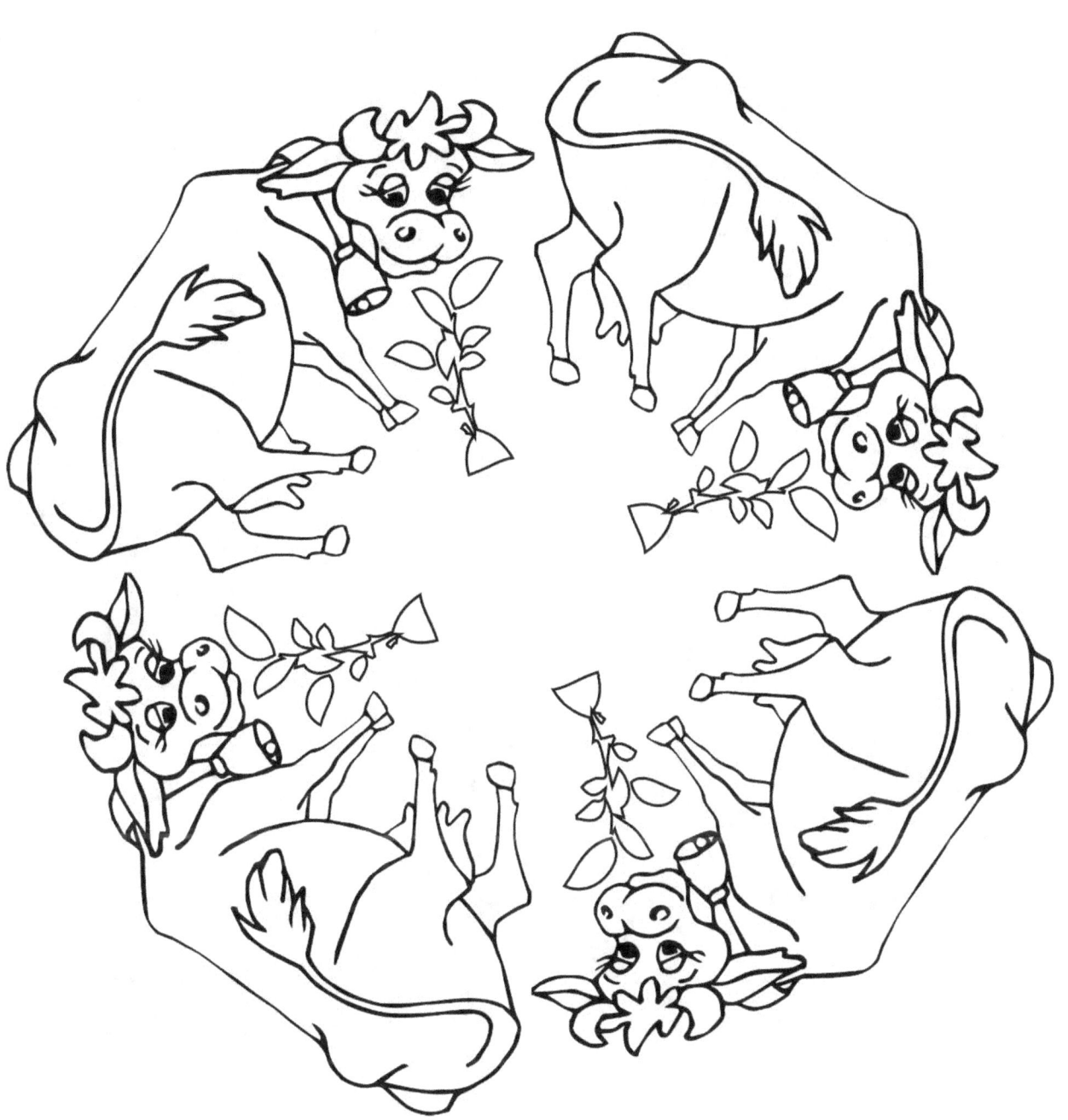